Ruth Lascelle

# ON WHAT DAY
# DID CHRIST DIE ?

# ON WHAT DAY
# DID CHRIST DIE ?

*The Last Week of Christ*

Revised Edition

by
## Ruth Specter Lascelle

𝕭
Bedrock Publishing
*Arlington, Washington*

**Library of Congress Cataloging-in-Publication Data**
Lascelle, Ruth Specter
On What Day Did Christ Die?: The Last Week of Christ/
Ruth Specter Lascelle.
   Understanding some contradictions in the last week
   of Christ. Includes biographical references and index.
      1. Three days and nights. 2. Scriptures listed of last
   week. 3. Charts and diagrams. 4. Jewish customs,
   counting of time. 5. The Passover system, burial, etc.
   6. Scroggie's errors/Appendix.

Library of Congress Catalog Card Number:  96-80198
                ISBN 0-9654519-9-2

First edition printed by Exposition Press, 1959


Printed in the United States of America
by

Bedrock Publishing
24824 Jim Creek Road
Arlington,WA 98223-6883
Fax: 360-403-0376

*Cover printed by Gorham Printing*
*Rochester, WA 98579*

*Dedicated to Bible students
in the hope that this book
may promote a study of the
last days of Christ on earth
and explain some difficulties
surrounding them
in the Gospel narrative.*

## Books by Ruth Specter Lascelle

The Passover Feast

On What Day Did Christ Die?: "The Last Week of Christ" (*revised*)

A Dwelling Place For God (*revised and enlarged*)

We Have a Great High Priest: "A Brief Study of The Book of Hebrews" *(revised)*

Jewish Faith and The New Covenant (formerly, "The Bud and The Flower of Judaism," *(revised)*

That They Might be Saved: "Eight Lessons in Jewish Evangelism"

Hanukkah and Christmas

Global Harvest (formerly, "Sent Forth by God," *revised*)

How Shall They Hear? (with Hyman Israel Specter)

God's Calendar of Prophetic Events: "Leviticus Twenty-Three"

Pictures of Messiah in The Holy Scriptures

Two Loaves—One Bread: "Jew and Gentile in the Church"

Jewish Love for a Gentile: "Story of The Lascelles"

New Covenant Passover Haggadah: "Remembering The Exodus of Deliverance"

# AUTHOR'S PREFACE

For almost 2,000 years after the crucifixion of Messiah, the day on which He died was not disputed, but recently it has been questioned whether the day was really Friday, since Friday could not be reconciled with a period of three days and three nights to Sunday, the day of His resurrection as it had been prophesied.

It is my prayer that this work will help the sincere reader to an understanding of this problem, as well as other seeming contradictions. Therefore I have included many of the customs of the New Testament times which clarify the meaning of this particular portion of the Gospel Story.

The first publisher of this work wrote: "The conclusions Mrs. Lascelle has reached are highly interesting and convincing. The combination of research, good detective work, deduction and argument have resulted in an exciting and believable treatise. Here, then, is a little book of immense interest for the student of religion and it is highly recommended to anyone who finds Biblical history, or any history for that matter, a fascinating study" (*Exposition Press, Inc.*, New York).

"On What Day Did Christ Die?" has been out of print for several years but the demand for it has prompted me to prepare it for republication. Several portions have been revised, material relevant to the subject with other interesting articles has been added and its format has been rearranged to make for easier reading. My desire is to feature in this volume the *accuracy of the Scriptures*, especially the fulfillment of the types and symbols concerning the last days of Christ on earth.

# Table of Contents

# CHAPTER ONE

## Introduction

### In the Heart of the Earth

*"Now the LORD had prepared a great fish* [sea monster] *to swallow up Jonah. And Jonah was in the belly of the fish three days and three nights"* (Jonah 1:17).

*"...and there shall no sign be given it but the sign of the prophet Jonas: For as Jonas was three days and three nights in the whale's belly* [belly of the sea-monster; Greek text]; *so shall the Son of man be three days and three nights in the heart of the earth"* (Matthew 12:39, 40).

The Bible tells us that before the resurrection of Christ, the spirit-soul left the body of the person who died and entered *"the heart of the earth," "the center of the earth."* The body was buried, burned, or entombed on or in the *surface* of the earth. The spirit of the wicked entered into *sheol* (Hebrew text), the section of torment, or *Gehenna*, and the righteous into the paradise section of *sheol*, or "Abraham's Bosom," the place of comfort.

On the day of the crucifixion, Christ said to the thief beside Him on another cross, *"...To day shalt thou be with me in paradise"* (Luke 23:43). That day was Nisan 14 according to the Jewish calendar. That very day at three o'clock in the afternoon (the ninth hour of Luke 23:44) the sun was darkened, the veil in the Temple was rent in the midst as Christ cried with a loud

1

voice, saying, *"...Father, into thy hands I commend my **spirit**: and having said thus, he gave up the **ghost**"* (Luke 23:46).

Solomon, who was given the wisdom of God, declared: *"There is no man that hath power over the **spirit** to retain the **spirit**; neither hath he power in the **day of death** ..."* (Ecclesiastes 8:8). Christ, who humbled Himself to partake of flesh and blood as a human (yet He was, and is Divine), did not hold back the spirit in the day of His death. His body "fell asleep" and was still on the cross, but He, Himself, "descended into the lower parts of the earth." The thief died later that day when the soldiers came and broke the bones of his legs. The thief's *body* was still on the cross, but he (that part of his being which "knows, thinks, feels, and remembers"), having occupied that house of flesh, immediately as he left it, also went down into the place of departed spirits. That very day (Nisan 14) the thief was with the Lord in Paradise even as the Lord had promised!

When Christ prophesied that He would be "in the heart of earth," He was speaking of *sheol* and He referred *not* to His *body*, but to His spirit-soul, for His body was laid in a tomb on the *surface* of the earth! (See Appendix I: "Scroggie's Errors".)

## Three Days and Three Nights

The Gospel writers declare that the purpose of Messiah in going to Jerusalem that last week was *to die* and *to rise on the third day*. From the Scriptures a great deal of emphasis was placed upon *the very hour* that the Lamb of God should be sacrificed, and this was fulfilled exactly as it was prophesied. The following schemes will show different time-schedules for Christ prophecy of His death, burial and resurrection:

Let us suppose that Christ was crucified on a Wednesday:

| | | |
|---|---|---|
| Wednesday | 3 p.m. until 12 p.m. | 9 hours |
| Thursday | 12 p.m. until 12 p.m. | 24 hours |
| Friday | 12 p.m. until 12 p.m. | 24 hours |
| Saturday | 12 p.m. until 12 p.m. | 24 hours |
| Sunday | 12 p.m. until 6 a.m. | 6 hours |
| | | 87 hours |

Total Time = Four incomplete days, four nights.

Let us suppose that Christ was crucified on a Thursday:

| | | |
|---|---|---|
| Thursday. | 3 p.m. until 12 p.m. | 9 hours |
| Friday | 12 p.m. until 12 p.m. | 24 hours |
| Saturday | 12 p.m. until 6 a.m. | 6 hours |
| | | 39 hours |

Total Time = Three incomplete days, three nights.

How can we reconcile the foregoing two schedules with the statement of our Lord concerning "three days and three nights"? We must realize that, in this expression, we are dealing with an Old Testament term which cannot be set down in Western speech or in Oriental tongue to mean a literal fulfillment extending to exactly 72 hours. The Greeks as well as the Jews of those days counted time differently than we do now.

## Definition of "Day"

In the very beginning, days[1] were considered *from the evening to morning*, the night preceding the day (Genesis 1:5,

---

[1]The word "day" is used in Scripture in three ways: (1) that part of the solar day of 24 hours which is light (Genesis 1:5, 14; John 9:4; 11:9); (2) such a day, set apart for some distinctive purpose, as, "day of atonement" (Leviticus 23:27); "day of judgment" (Matthew 10:15); (3) a period of time, long or short, during which certain revealed purposes of God are to be accomplished, as "day of the LORD."

8, 13, 19, 23, 31). Furthermore, the term "day" obviously had two senses as night and day, or day contrasted with night. And though the day is mentioned first, this does not necessarily mean the time which was *light*, for the Jews counted from the *dark* part of the day (evening or sunset).[2]

> *"And it came to pass, when David and his men were come to Ziklag **on the third day,** ..."* (1 Samuel 30:1).

> *"... for he had eaten no bread, nor drunk any water, **three days and three nights"*** (1 Samuel 30:12).

> *"... because **three days ago** I fell sick"* (1 Samuel 30:13).

In the foregoing verses of Scripture, referring also to the context, we find that the expressions "third day," "three *days* and three *nights*," and "three *days* ago" are used to signify the same period of time.

> *"Go, gather together all the Jews that are present in Shushan, and fast ye for me, and neither eat nor drink **three days, night or day:** ..."* (Esther 4:16).

> *"Now it came to pass on the **third day**, that Esther put on her royal apparel, and stood in the inner court of the king's house, ..."* (Esther 5:1).

These two verses indicate that the phrase "three days, *night* and *day*" is used in conjunction with and equivalent to the phrase "*on* the third day." And though the third day itself was not completed, it was counted as a period of "three days and three nights."

> *"And they pitched one over against the other **seven days**. And so it was, that **in** the seventh day the battle was joined: ..."*

---

[2]The use of "evening" and "morning" may be held to limit "day" to the solar day; but the frequent parabolic use of natural phenomena may warrant the conclusion that each creative "day" was a period of time marked off by a beginning and ending.

(1 Kings 20:29). Here it is plain to see that it was not a complete seven days intended.

Time is not very definite as to its exact duration to the Jewish people. In the days of Christ "the accuracy of our measurement of time had no existence."

In the Jews' Talmud, Rabbi Eleazar ben Azaryah, who was tenth in descent from Ezra, said: "A day and a night are an *Onah* and the portion of an Onah[3] is as the whole of it."[4] If a Jewish boy is born in the last hour or even in the last few minutes of a day, it is counted as a complete day of the eight days within which he must be circumcised.

*Hermeneutics*[5] gives the term *synecdoche*[6] as a figure which receives something from one word to the other, two ideas that connect. Synecdoche of the three days is where the three days is put for the three nights. Synecdoche of the three nights is where the three nights is put for the three days.

The following quotations might clarify the expression, 'three days and three nights.'

(1) "Not three whole days and nights but part of three natural days, *nuchthumeron* or **night-day**, the Greeks called them … it is a manner of speech very usual."[7]

(2) "The Greek text usually translated 'in three days' is really interpreted correctly as 'inside of three days' or 'within three days.'

(3) "Reckoning the parts only of the first and last days. Thus the Greeks commonly speak of 'three days ago' when they mean that *a day only* intervened."[8]

---

[3]Hebrew word meaning "a portion of time."

[4]*J. Shabbath* 9:3. Also *B. Pesachim* 4a.

[5]Hermeneutics is the principles of biblical interpretation (from Heremes, the messenger of the Greek deities).

[6]A figure of speech in which a part stands for the whole or the whole for a part.

[7]*Matthew Henry's Commentary*, Vol. 5, page 176.

[8]Rev. Ingram Cobbin, M.A., *Bible Dictionary.*

(4) The Jews spoke of a 'day and a night' as a unit which they did not divide into parts when considering 'days.' Therefore three times 'a day and a night' would only be *one whole day with parts of two others.*[9]

(5) "Three days and three nights–probably, like the antitype, Messiah, Jonah was cast forth on the land **on** *the third day* (Matthew 12:40), the Hebrew counting the first and third parts of days as whole 24 hour days."[10]

(6) "'Three days and three nights' was a familiar idiomatic phrase to cover a period that included any part of three days. Though this may puzzle a theological college, no prison chaplain would need to explain it to his congregation. For our law reckons time on this same system. Though our legal day is a day and a night (24 hours beginning at midnight), any part of a day counts as a day. Therefore, under the sentence of three days' imprisonment a prisoner is usually discharged on the morning of the third day, no matter how late on the first day he reaches the prison. Under such a sentence a prisoner is seldom more than 40 hours in *gaol* [prison], and I have had official cognizance of cases where the detention was, in fact, only for 33 hours. And this mode of reckoning and of speaking was as familiar to the Jews as it is to our prison officials and the habitués of our criminal courts."[11]

The unbelieving Jews, to whom Christ used the expression of *'three days and three nights,'* did not understand it to signify a period of 72 hours as we use it today, for after He had been crucified, they came to Pilate, *"Saying, Sir, we remember that that deceiver said, while he was yet alive, **After** three days I will rise again. Command therefore that the sepulchre be made sure **until** the third day. ..."* (Matthew 27:63-64). "The fact that

---

[9] See Matthew 16:21 with Mark 8:31; 2 Chronicles 10:5 with 10:12; Esther 4:16 with 5:1.

[10] *Jamieson, Fausset, and Brown Commentary*, p. 634.

[11] Sir Robert Anderson.

'three days' is used by Hebrew idiom for any part of three days and three nights is not disputed: because that was the common way of reckoning, just as it was when used of years."[12]

Christ said He would rise from the dead *on* the third day. The phrase '*on* the third day' cannot mean other than that the resurrection took place on *that* day, for, if it occurred *after* the third day, it would be on the *fourth* day and not the third! The phrase 'after three days' is used by the same writers (Matthew and Luke) in connection with the 'third day' as meaning the same thing. *On the **third** day* cannot mean *on the **fourth** day*, while ***after** three days* can be used as meaning ***on** the third day*. *"And it came to pass **after** seven days, that the waters of the flood were upon the earth"* (Genesis 7:10). In present-day thinking, ***after** seven days* would mean *the eighth day*, but the Hebrew tells us it is ***on** the seventh day*.

Knowing about the well-known custom of the Jews in counting a part of a day as a whole day-and-night period, their days beginning at sunset and ending at sunset, along with the Old Testament term 'three days and three nights', helps us to understand the time element of Messiah's descent 'into the heart of the earth.'

---

Let us suppose then that Christ was crucified on a Friday and calculate by the Jewish reckoning:

Friday:           3 p.m. until 6 p.m.  (1 day)  =  1st day

Saturday: (Friday) 6 p.m. until 6 p.m.  (2 days) =  2nd day

Sunday:(Saturday) 6 p.m. until 6 a.m.  (3 days) =  3rd day

---

The above schedule would be ***three days and three nights*** according to the Old Testament usage of the term!

---

[12]*The Companion Bible.*

7

# CHAPTER TWO
# Last Days of Christ
# Harmonized in The Gospels

## SECTION 1
## NISAN 9 TO NISAN 13

**SUNDAY, NISAN 9 (Saturday evening)**

FROM JERICHO TO BETHANY/SIX DAYS BEFORE THE PASSOVER

### John 12:1

1. *Then Jesus six days before the passover came to Bethany, where Lazarus was which had been dead, whom he raised from the dead.*

Geographically the town of Bethany is located on the Mount of Olives, but *fully a mile beyond the summit*, on the eastern slope, i.e., the side away from Jerusalem. *"Then returned they unto Jerusalem from the **mount called Olivet**, which is from Jerusalem **a sabbath day's journey"** (Acts 1:12). A sabbath day's journey is *six furlongs* or a little less than a mile. *"Now Bethany was nigh unto Jerusalem, about fifteen furlongs off"* (John 11:18). This verse locates Bethany (the *actual city*, not the geographical boundary) as 15 furlongs, or *two miles,* from Jerusalem.

By comparing John's statement with the events leading up to the seven-day observance listed in the Gospels, Nisan 9 was six days before the Passover *Feast*, which was legally observed (after the *Paschal **sacrifice*** of Nisan 14) at the beginning of

*Nisan 15.* The Passover was the day of Sacrifice (Nisan 14) as well as the whole period of seven days which began on Nisan 15.

## MONDAY, NISAN 10 (Sunday evening)

**JESUS IS ANOINTED BY MARY AT SUPPER**

### *Matthew 26:6-13*

6. *Now when Jesus was in Bethany, in the house of Simon the leper,*
7. *There came unto him a woman having an alabaster box of very precious ointment, and poured it on his head, as he sat at meat.*
8. *But when his disciples saw it, they had indignation, saying, To what purpose is this waste?*
9. *For this ointment might have been sold for much, and given to the poor.*
10. *When Jesus understood it, he said unto them, Why trouble ye the woman? for she hath wrought a good work upon me.*
11. *For ye have the poor always with you; but me ye have not always.*
12. *For in that she hath poured this ointment on my body, she did it for my burial.*
13. *Verily I say unto you, Wheresoever this gospel shall be preached in the whole world, there shall also this, that this woman hath done, be told for a memorial of her.*

### *Mark 14:3-9*

3. *And being in Bethany in the house of Simon the leper, as he sat at meat, there came a woman having an alabaster box of ointment of spikenard very precious; and she brake the box, and poured it on his head.*

4. *And there were some that had indignation within themselves, and said, Why was this waste of the ointment made?*

5. *For it might have been sold for more than three hundred pence, and have been given to the poor. And they murmured against her.*

6. *And Jesus said, Let her alone; why trouble ye her? she hath wrought a good work on me.*

7. *For ye have the poor with you always, and whensoever ye will ye may do them good: but me ye have not always.*

8. *She hath done what she could: she is come aforehand to anoint my body to the burying.* [While He was yet alive His body was anointed because there would be no time for this after His death.]

9. *Verily I say unto you, Wheresoever this gospel shall be preached throughout the whole world, this also that she hath done shall be spoken of for a memorial of her.*

### *John 12:2-3*

2. *There they made him a supper; and Martha served: but Lazarus was one of them that sat at the table with him.*

3. *Then took Mary a pound of ointment of spikenard, very costly, and anointed the feet of Jesus, and wiped his feet with her hair: and the house was filled with the odour of the ointment.*

"She anointed both His feet and His head. The Holy Spirit reports the anointing of the head of the Lord in Matthew, because this is in harmony with the object of the Gospel. He is the King, and while He is the rejected King, her [Mary's] faith no doubt looked beyond death and burial. The Holy Spirit gives the anointing of the feet and leaves out the anointing of the head, because the King is the Son of God; as such He is described in the Gospel of John, and that attitude of Mary before His feet anointing them is in fullest harmony with the fourth Gospel."[13]

---

[13]A.C. Gaebelein, *The Annotated Bible*, Vol.1.

## John 12:4-8

4. *Then saith one of his disciples, Judas Iscariot, Simon's son, which should betray him,*
5. *Why was not this ointment sold for three hundred pence, and given to the poor?*
6. *This he said, not that he cared for the poor; but because he was a thief, and had the bag, and bare what was put therein.*
7. *Then said Jesus, Let her alone: against the day of my burying hath she kept this.*
8. *For the poor always ye have with you; but me ye have not always.*

**CROWDS COME TO SEE JESUS AND LAZARUS**

## John 12:9

9. *Much people of the Jews therefore knew that he was there: and they came not for Jesus' sake only, but that they might see Lazarus also, whom he had raised from the dead.*

This miracle of raising Lazarus from the dead attracted the Jews to see the Miracle-Worker as well as the one He raised up. Many of the Jewish people believed as they saw the miracle. This angered the religious leaders against Jesus all the more. They could not deny that one who was dead now was alive, for they saw it with their own eyes. Jesus predicted that this would happen, i.e., that though one were raised from the dead, they would not believe (Luke 16:31).

**KING REJECTED AND SET ASIDE AS LAMB**

## Matthew 26:14-16

14. *Then one of the twelve, called Judas Iscariot, went unto the chief priests,*

15. And said unto them, *What will ye give me, and I will deliver him unto you?* And they covenanted with him for thirty pieces of silver.

16. And from that time he sought opportunity to betray him.

### Mark 14:10-11

10. And Judas Iscariot, one of the twelve, went unto the chief priests, to betray him unto them.

11. And when they heard it, they were glad, and promised to give him money. And he sought how he might conveniently betray him.

### Luke 22:1-6

1. Now the feast of unleavened bread drew nigh, which is called the Passover.

2. And the chief priests and scribes sought how they might kill him; for they feared the people.

3. Then entered Satan into Judas surnamed Iscariot, being of the number of the twelve.

4. And he went his way, and communed with the chief priests and captains, how he might betray him unto them.

5. And they were glad, and covenanted to give him money.

6. And he promised, and sought opportunity to betray him unto them in the absence of the multitude.

## MONDAY, NISAN 10 (Monday morning)

### FROM BETHANY TO JERUSALEM/THE TRIUMPHAL ENTRY

### Matthew 21:1-11

1. And when they drew nigh unto Jerusalem, and were come to Bethphage, unto the mount of Olives, then sent Jesus two disciples,

2. *Saying unto them, Go into the village over against you, and straightway ye shall find an ass tied, and a colt with her: loose them, and bring them unto me.*

3. *And if any man say ought unto you, ye shall say, The Lord hath need of them; and straightway he will send them.*

4. *All this was done, that it might be fulfilled which was spoken by the prophet, saying,*

5. *Tell ye the daughter of Sion, Behold, thy King cometh unto thee, meek, and sitting upon an ass, and a colt the foal of an ass.*

6. *And the disciples went, and did as Jesus commanded them,*

7. *And brought the ass, and the colt, and put on them their clothes, and they set him thereon.*

8. *And a very great multitude spread their garments in the way; others cut down branches from the trees, and strowed them in the way.*

9. *And the multitudes that went before, and that followed, cried, saying, Hosanna to the son of David: Blessed is he that cometh in the name of the Lord; Hosanna in the highest.*

10. *And when he was come into Jerusalem, all the city was moved, saying, Who is this?*

11. *And the multitude said, This is Jesus the prophet of Nazareth of Galilee.*

### *Mark 11:1-10*

1. *And when they came nigh to Jerusalem, unto Bethphage and Bethany, at the mount of Olives, he sendeth forth two of his disciples,*

2. *And saith unto them, Go your way into the village over against you: and as soon as ye be entered into it, ye shall find a colt tied, whereon never man sat; loose him, and bring him.*

3. *And if any man say unto you, Why do ye this? say ye that the Lord hath need of him; and straightway he will send him hither.*

4. *And they went their way, and found the colt tied by the door without in a place where two ways met; and they loose him.*

5. *And certain of them that stood there said unto them, What do ye, loosing the colt?*

6. *And they said unto them even as Jesus had commanded: and they let them go.*

7. *And they brought the colt to Jesus, and cast their garments on him; and he sat upon him.*

8. *And many spread their garments in the way: and others cut down branches off the trees, and strowed them in the way.*

9. *And they that went before, and they that followed, cried, saying, Hosanna; Blessed is he that cometh in the name of the Lord:*

10. *Blessed be the kingdom of our father David, that cometh in the name of the Lord: Hosanna in the highest.*

Note: The words, "Blessed is he that cometh in the name of the Lord", relate to the Messiah and is used by orthodox Jews on several religious occasions, particularly in the wedding ceremony!

### *Luke 19:29-38*

29. *And it came to pass, when he was come nigh to Bethphage and Bethany, at the mount called the mount of Olives, he sent two of his disciples,*

30. *Saying, Go ye into the village over against you; in the which at your entering ye shall find a colt tied, whereon yet never man sat: loose him, and bring him hither.*

31. *And if any man ask you, Why do ye loose him? thus shall ye say unto him, Because the Lord hath need of him.*

32. *And they that were sent went their way, and found even as he had said unto them.*

33. *And as they were loosing the colt, the owners thereof said unto them, Why loose ye the colt?*

34. *And they said, The Lord hath need of him.*

35. *And they brought him to Jesus: and they cast their garments upon the colt, and they set Jesus thereon.*

36. *And as he went, they spread their clothes in the way.*

37. *And when he was come nigh, even now at the descent of the mount of Olives, the whole multitude of the disciples began to rejoice and praise God with a loud voice for all the mighty works that they had seen;*

38. *Saying, Blessed be the King that cometh in the name of the Lord: peace in heaven, and glory in the highest.*

### John 12:12-13

12. *On the next day much people that were come to the feast, when they heard that Jesus was coming to Jerusalem,*

13. *Took branches of palm trees, and went forth to meet him, and cried, Hosanna: Blessed is the King of Israel that cometh in the name of the Lord.*

Jesus would not travel from Jericho to Bethany (16 miles) or from Bethany to Jerusalem (two miles) on the *Sabbath* day. Therefore Nisan 9 could only fall on *Sunday* and Nisan 10 on *Monday*. Thus we see that the Triumphal Entry occurred on Monday, not on Sunday, as is usually held. This arrangement does away with the awkward "day of silence" so often indicated by chronologists of Passion Week.

"Much people"–Some ancient authorities read *the common people*. Though the common people hailed Jesus as their King, the religious leaders of the Jews, who were representatives of the nation, rejected Him as such and decreed that He be executed. The instant they refused Him as King, they automatically set Him aside as God's Lamb, appointing Him to death. According to the prophecy, the chief priests set the price and took to them *a lamb on the tenth of Nisan* which, in the law, *must* occur at that time (see Exodus 12:3)!

### John 12:14-18

14. *And Jesus, when he had found a young ass, sat thereon; as it is written,*

15. *Fear not, daughter of Sion: behold, thy King cometh, sitting on an ass's colt.*

16. *These things understood not his disciples at the first: but when Jesus was glorified, then remembered they that these things were written of him, and that they had done these things unto him.*

17. *The people therefore that was with him when he called Lazarus out of his grave, and raised him from the dead, bare record.*

18. *For this cause the people also met him, for that they heard that he had done this miracle.*

## TUESDAY, NISAN 11 (Monday evening)

### RETURN TO BETHANY

### *Matthew 21:17*

17. *And he left them, and went out of the city into Bethany; and he lodged there.*

### *Mark 11:11*

11. *And Jesus entered into Jerusalem, and into the temple: and when he had looked round about upon all things, and now the eventide was come, he went out unto Bethany with the twelve.*

## TUESDAY, NISAN 11 (Tuesday morning)

### FROM BETHANY TO JERUSALEM

### *Matthew 21:18*

18. *Now in the morning as he returned into the city, he hungered.*

## Mark 11:12

12. And on the morrow, when they were come from Bethany, he was hungry:

**FIG TREE CURSED**

## Matthew 21:19

19. And when he saw a fig tree in the way, he came to it, and found nothing thereon, but leaves only, and said unto it, Let no fruit grow on thee henceforward for ever. And presently the fig tree withered away.

## Mark 11:13-14

13. And seeing a fig tree afar off having leaves, he came, if haply he might find any thing thereon: and when he came to it, he found nothing but leaves; for the time of figs was not yet.
14. And Jesus answered and said unto it, No man eat fruit of thee hereafter for ever. And his disciples heard it.

**CLEANSING OF THE TEMPLE**

## Matthew 21:12-13

12. And Jesus went into the temple of God, and cast out all them that sold and bought in the temple, and overthrew the tables of the moneychangers, and the seats of them that sold doves,
13. And said unto them, It is written, My house shall be called the house of prayer[14]; but ye have made it a den of thieves.

---

[14]Hebrew rendering is: "the house of **my** prayer." See Isaiah 56:7.

*15. And they come to Jerusalem: and Jesus went into the temple, and began to cast out them that sold and bought in the temple, and overthrew the tables of the moneychangers, and the seats of them that sold doves;*

*16. And would not suffer that any man should carry any vessel through the temple.*

*17. And he taught, saying unto them, Is it not written, My house shall be called of all nations the house of prayer? but ye have made it a den of thieves.*

"The cleansing of the Temple should be placed as stated by Mark, for the following reasons:

"(a) Matthew is far more prone to ignore chronological sequence than Mark, especially in matters pertaining to the last week. Combining events is typical of Matthew.

"(b) Mark gives a very concise detailed chronological account of each day's happenings for the entire interval between the triumphal entry and the crucifixion, a thing which Matthew does not attempt.

"(c) Matthew is writing of Jesus as the 'King of the Jews.' In this capacity Jesus had the responsibility and authority (and demonstrated it) as King, to cleanse the Temple. (The last king of Israel to exercise this prerogative was Josiah, recorded in 2 Kings 23:4.) Hence the account of the cleansing of the Temple belongs in Matthew's account exactly where Matthew places it, on the day that Jesus manifested His kingship, *regardless of when it actually occurred.* It would have been out of place when Jesus was but a rejected king and a 'set-aside lamb.'

"(d) Luke does not differentiate between the different days with their accompanying events and teachings, preferring to include everything in one grand whole. Hence obviously he does not intend to state chronological happenings."[15]

---

[15]Roy M. Allen, *Three Days in the Grave.*

## Luke 19:45-46

45. And he went into the temple, and began to cast out them that sold therein, and them that bought;
46. Saying unto them, It is written, My house is the house of prayer: but ye have made it a den of thieves.

## John 2:14-17

14. And found in the temple those that sold oxen and sheep and doves, and the changers of money sitting:
15. And when he had made a scourge of small cords, he drove them all out of the temple, and the sheep, and the oxen; and poured out the changers' money, and overthrew the tables;
16. And said unto them that sold doves, Take these things hence; make not my Father's house an house of merchandise.
17. And his disciples remembered that it was written, The zeal of thine house hath eaten me up.[16]

# WEDNESDAY, NISAN 12 (Tuesday evening)

**LEAVES JERUSALEM FOR BETHANY**

## Mark 11:19

19. And when even was come, he went out of the city.

**FROM BETHANY TO JERUSALEM/FIG TREE FOUND DEAD**

## Matthew 21:20-22

20. And when the disciples saw it, they marvelled, saying, How soon is the fig tree withered away!
21. Jesus answered and said unto them, Verily I say unto you, If ye have faith, and doubt not, ye shall not only do this which is

---

[16]Psalm 69:9.

done to the fig tree, but also if ye shall say unto this mountain, Be thou removed, and be thou cast into the sea; it shall be done.

22. And all things, whatsoever ye shall ask in prayer, believing, ye shall receive.

## Mark 11:20-25

20. And in the morning, as they passed by, they saw the fig tree dried up from the roots.

21. And Peter calling to remembrance saith unto him, Master, behold, the fig tree which thou cursedst is withered away.

22. And Jesus answering saith unto them, Have faith in God.

23. For verily I say unto you, That whosoever shall say unto this mountain, Be thou removed, and be thou cast into the sea; and shall not doubt in his heart, but shall believe that those things which he saith shall come to pass; he shall have whatsoever he saith.

24. Therefore I say unto you, What things soever ye desire, when ye pray, believe that ye receive them, and ye shall have them.

25. And when ye stand praying, forgive, if ye have ought against any: that your Father also which is in heaven may forgive you your trespasses.

**TO MOUNT OF OLIVES**

## Matthew 24:1-3

1. And Jesus went out, and departed from the temple: and his disciples came to him for to show him the buildings of the temple.

2. And Jesus said unto them, See ye not all these things? verily I say unto you, There shall not be left here one stone upon another, that shall not be thrown down.

3. And as he sat upon the mount of Olives, the disciples came unto him privately, saying, Tell us, when shall these things be? and what shall be the sign of thy coming, and of the end of the world?

## Mark 13:1-4

1. *And as he went out of the temple, one of his disciples saith unto him, Master, see what manner of stones and what buildings are here!*
2. *And Jesus answering said unto him, Seest thou these great buildings? there shall not be left one stone upon another, that shall not be thrown down.*
3. *And as he sat upon the mount of Olives over against the temple, Peter and James and John and Andrew asked him privately,*
4. *Tell us, when shall these things be? and what shall be the sign when all these things shall be fulfilled?*

**THE OLIVET DISCOURSE**

Matthew 24, 25

Mark 13

Luke 21:15-36

**AFTER TWO DAYS IS PASSOVER**

## Matthew 26:1-2

1. *And it came to pass, when Jesus had finished all these sayings, he said unto his disciples,*
2. *Ye know that **after two days** is the feast of the passover, and the Son of man is betrayed to be crucified.*

## Mark 14:1

1. ***After two days** was the feast of the passover, and of unleavened bread: and the chief priests and the scribes sought how they might take him by craft, and put him to death.*

Toward evening Messiah informed His disciples that it would be *in two days* He would be betrayed. In other words: 'after two days,' 'in two days,' 'on the second day from now' (to be consistent with Jewish reckoning, or 'day after tomorrow' as we would say today), the time to offer the Paschal lamb would come and Messiah would be delivered up for execution.

In the statement of Mark and Matthew "*feast of the*" are words supplied by the translators. The *day* of the Passover sacrifice was Nisan 14 (Friday). Messiah prophesied that He would be betrayed on this *day*. We notice by the account in the Gospels that it was after supper in the Garden of Gethsemane when Messiah was apprehended after the "kiss of Judas." Since the Jews counted the day from sunset, this occurred in the beginning hours of Nisan 14, the time Messiah foretold!

The Scriptures emphasize the day and exact time for the betrayal, the trial, the crucifixion, the burial and resurrection of the Messiah! Accordingly–it was carried out as God had planned it from before the foundation of the world!

## THURSDAY, NISAN 13 (Wednesday evening)

### JESUS STAYS IN THE MOUNT ALL NIGHT

### *Luke 21:37*

*37. And in the day time he was teaching in the temple; and at night he went out, and abode in the mount that is called the mount of Olives.*

### DISCIPLES ASK WHERE TO PREPARE THE PASSOVER

### *Matthew 26:17*

*17. Now the first day of the feast of unleavened bread the disciples came to Jesus, saying unto him, Where wilt thou that we prepare for thee to eat the passover?*

12. *And the first day of unleavened bread, when they killed the passover, his disciples said unto him, Where wilt thou that we go and prepare that thou mayest eat the passover?*

The Passover Feast and the Feast of Unleavened Bread were contained in *one* Feast (see Luke 22:1). According to *Josephus*, (*Ant*.iii.10,5), the Passover Feast began yearly on the fourteenth day of the first moon in the Jewish month Abib (Nisan), and it lasted only one day; but it was immediately followed by the "days of unleavened bread," which were seven. So that the whole lasted *eight* days, and all the eight days are sometimes called, "the feast of the passover," and sometimes "the feast (or days) of unleavened bread" (see Leviticus 23:5-6).

*"Thou shalt not offer the blood of my sacrifice with* (literally, **upon**) *leaven; ..."* (Exodus 34:25).

*"Seven days shall ye eat unleavened bread; even the first day **ye shall have put away** leaven out of your houses: for whosoever eateth leavened bread from the first day until the seventh day, that soul shall be cut off from Israel"* (Exodus 12:15; *Isaac Leeser's* translation.)

The Jews were to have *already* removed the leaven by the day of the Passover sacrifice, Nisan 14. This necessitated the purchase of unleavened bread on Nisan 13. In the Talmud we find an interesting law and ritual of the Pharisees: "On the evening before Nisan 14 [this would be Nisan 13] before the coming out of the stars, they are to search for the leaven by the light of a single wax taper."[17] "By way of public notification, two desecrated thank offering cakes were laid on a bench in the Temple, the removal of one of which indicated that the time for

_____

[17]*Passover Prayers,* fol.1, Col.2.

eating what was leavened was past; the removal of the other, that the time for destroying all leaven had come."[18]

The threat of being cut off from Israel was taken so seriously that it was the universal practice to put away leaven *a whole day before* the prescribed period, i.e., on the 13th instead of the 14th. This is common among orthodox Jews to this time. My mother and grandmother observed this practice and we began to eat the unleavened bread on Nisan 13. This particular custom, which was made by the Jewish religious leaders, but ordained by God, provided unleavened bread for the use of Jesus on the occasion of the Last Supper with His disciples. He must have unleavened bread for, in speaking of the bread which He took in His hands and broke, He said: *"...This is my body which is given for you..."* (Luke 22:19). Nothing but *unleavened* bread could properly symbolize His *sinless* body! So we paraphrase the verses (Matthew 26:17, Mark 14:12, Luke 22:7) and tie them in with Jewish custom: "And on the first day when the Jews begin to eat unleavened bread (Nisan 13, a whole day ahead), which is related to the day for the sacrifice of the Passover lamb (on Nisan 14), ... etc."

### *Luke 22:7-9*

7. *Then came the day of unleavened bread, when the passover must be killed.*
8. *And he sent Peter and John, saying, Go and prepare us the passover, that we may eat.*
9. *And they said unto him, Where wilt thou that we prepare?*

---

[18]*Jerusalem Talmud.*

## Matthew 26:18-19

18. *And he said, Go into the city to such a man, and say unto him, The Master saith, My time is at hand; I will keep the passover at thy house with my disciples.*

19. *And the disciples did as Jesus had appointed them; and they made ready the passover.*

## Mark 14:13-16

13. *And he sendeth forth two of his disciples, and saith unto them, Go ye into the city, and there shall meet you a man bearing a pitcher of water: follow him.*

14. *And wheresoever he shall go in, say ye to the goodman of the house, The Master saith, Where is the guestchamber, where I shall eat the passover with my disciples?*

15. *And he will show you a large upper room furnished and prepared: there make ready for us.*

16. *And his disciples went forth, and came into the city, and found as he had said unto them: and they made ready the passover.*

## Luke 22:10-13

10. *And he said unto them, Behold, when ye are entered into the city, there shall a man meet you, bearing a pitcher of water; follow him into the house where he entereth in.*

11. *And ye shall say unto the goodman of the house, The Master saith unto thee, Where is the guestchamber, where I shall eat the passover with my disciples?*

12. *And he shall show you a large upper room furnished: there make ready.*

13. *And they went, and found as he had said unto them: and they made ready the passover.*

Peter and John, according to the custom, would go to the Temple and provide for the lamb, which they must purchase and take to the priests who had to pass upon it. Early in the afternoon[19] the lamb would be killed in the Temple court, offered at the altar, and after the blood was poured out at the altar, and a certain part of the lamb was reserved for the sacrifice, the rest would be wrapped in the skin and taken home. Before sunset the carcass would be roasted in barbecue fashion (transfixed on a cross-shaped bar) and made ready for the meal at the blasts of the trumpet just at sunset. The apostles provided the wine, unleavened cakes, bitter herbs, and the charoseth or paste of crushed fruits moistened with vinegar, which represented the clay with which the Israelites made brick in Egypt. (A copy of *charoseth* is used in the Passover service or *Seder* of the Jews today!)

---

[19]See Exodus 12:6, "in the evening." The Hebrew rendering is "between the evenings," our 3 p.m.

# SECTION 2
# THE DAY OF THE CRUCIFIXION

## FRIDAY, NISAN 14 (Thursday evening)

### THE LAST SUPPER

### *Matthew 26:20-29*

20. *Now when the even was come, he sat down with the twelve.*
21. *And as they did eat, he said, Verily I say unto you, that one of you shall betray me.*
22. *And they were exceeding sorrowful, and began every one of them to say unto him, Lord, is it I?*
23. *And he answered and said, He that dippeth his hand with me in the dish, the same shall betray me.*
24. *The Son of man goeth as it is written of him: but woe unto that man by whom the Son of man is betrayed! it had been good for that man if he had not been born.*
25. *Then Judas, which betrayed him, answered and said, Master, is it I? He said unto him, Thou hast said.*
26. *And as they were eating, Jesus took bread, and blessed it, and brake it, and gave it to the disciples, and said, Take, eat; this is my body.*
27. *And he took the cup, and gave thanks, and gave it to them, saying, Drink ye all of it;*
28. *For this is my blood of the new testament, which is shed for many for the remission of sins.*
29. *But I say unto you, I will not drink henceforth of this fruit of the vine, until that day when I drink it new with you in my Father's kingdom.*

After the disciples had observed the Jewish traditional regulations which included the examination of the lamb by the priest and its being declared "spotless" (according to Jewish history it had to pass 52 points of inspection), roasting of the lamb as prescribed by God's commandment, buying that which was necessary for the feast, searching the "furnished" room (which had already been prepared) for any leaven according to the law of the Pharisees, Messiah participated in this meal with them. It is called a supper and He called it the Passover, but it is *not* the legal Passover Feast of the Jews. In John, during the "supper," Jesus told Judas to do that quickly which he had to do and the disciples misunderstood this: *"For some of them thought, because Judas had the* [money] *bag, that Jesus said unto him, Buy those things that we have need of against the feast; ..."* (John 13:29). This implies that the actual Feast of the Passover was to be on the following day.

When the disciples asked where to prepare for the Passover they thought that it was to be eaten by them and the Master at the same time with the rest of the Jews on the following day. However, Messiah gave directions for that very evening because He knew that the usual hour when the Passover Feast would be legally observed would be too late for them. They would partake of the Passover "before I suffer," Messiah said.

"The Lord did not eat his last Passover on the *legal day* of the Passover, but on the previous day, *the 13th*, and suffered on the day following, being Himself the Passover."[20]

"It was necessary for Jesus to observe the Passover festival one day in advance of the usual date beginning at sunset of Nisan the thirteenth or at the opening of Nisan fourteenth. *Under justifiable circumstances*, it was customary among the Jews of Messiah's day to eat the Passover *one day ahead of the appointed date*, and this is what Jesus did."[21]

---

[20]Clement of Alexandria [Fragment from '*Chron. Paschal,*' p. 14, edit. Dindorf].
[21]C. P. Roney, *Commentary on the Harmony of the Gospels.*

## Mark 14:17-25

*17. And in the evening he cometh with the twelve.*

*18. And as they sat and did eat, Jesus said, Verily I say unto you, One of you which eateth with me shall betray me.*

*19. And they began to be sorrowful, and to say unto him one by one, Is it I? and another said, Is it I?*

*20. And he answered and said unto them, It is one of the twelve, that dippeth with me in the dish.*

*21. The Son of man indeed goeth, as it is written of him: but woe to that man by whom the Son of man is betrayed! good were it for that man if he had never been born.*

*22. And as they did eat, Jesus took bread, and blessed, and brake it, and gave to them, and said, Take, eat: this is my body.*

*23. And he took the cup, and when he had given thanks, he gave it to them: and they all drank of it.*

*24. And he said unto them, This is my blood of the new testament, which is shed for many.*

*25. Verily I say unto you, I will drink no more of the fruit of the vine, until that day that I drink it new in the kingdom of God.*

## Luke 22:14-23

*14. And when the hour was come, he sat down, and the twelve apostles with him.*

*15. And he said unto them, With desire I have desired to eat this passover with you before I suffer:*

*16. For I say unto you, I will not any more eat thereof, until it be fulfilled in the kingdom of God.*

*17. And he took the cup, and gave thanks, and said, Take this, and divide it among yourselves:*

*18. For I say unto you, I will not drink of the fruit of the vine, until the kingdom of God shall come.*

*19. And he took bread, and gave thanks, and brake it, and gave unto them, saying, This is my body which is given for you: this do in remembrance of me.*

*20. Likewise also the cup after supper, saying, This cup is the new testament in my blood, which is shed for you.*

*21. But, behold, the hand of him that betrayeth me is with me on the table.*

*22. And truly the Son of man goeth, as it was determined: but woe unto that man by whom he is betrayed!*

*23. And they began to inquire among themselves, which of them it was that should do this thing.*

Messiah, of necessity, partook of a Passover meal before the legal Feast of the Jews for He must be the *true* Passover the next day to fulfill the type. He had eaten with His disciples at three Passover Feasts on the three preceding years since His public ministry, but this particular Feast He could not partake of in the same way and at the legal time, for this fourth one is to be the fulfillment of all the Passover Feasts before it by the shedding of His blood (laying down of His life) as the true Passover Lamb, and His body broken as the true Unleavened Bread. (Although Messiah did not eat at the legal Passover time with His disciples that year, He had this *anticipatory meal,* which He called a Passover, with them on the 14th of Nisan, the *day of the Passover sacrifice!*) "On the day of the Passover ye took him, and on the day of the Passover ye crucified him."[22]

### *John 13:1-9*

*1. Now **before the feast of the passover**, when Jesus knew that his hour was come that he should depart out of this world unto the Father, having loved his own which were in the world, he loved them unto the end.*

*2. **And supper being ended**, the devil having now put into the heart of Judas Iscariot, Simon's son, to betray him;*

*3. Jesus knowing that the Father had given all things into his hands, and that he was come from God, and went to God;*

---

[22]Justin Martyr: [Dial, cum Trypho, ch. iii], to the same effect write Irenaeus ['Adv. Haer', iv.23] and Tertullian ['Adv. Judaeos,' ch. 8].

4. *He riseth from supper, and laid aside his garments; and took a towel, and girded himself.*

5. *After that he poureth water into a basin, and began to wash the disciples' feet, and to wipe them with the towel wherewith he was girded.*

6. *Then cometh he to Simon Peter: and Peter saith unto him, Lord, dost thou wash my feet?*

7. *Jesus answered and said unto him, What I do thou knowest not now; but thou shalt know hereafter.*

8. *Peter saith unto him, Thou shalt never wash my feet. Jesus answered him, If I wash thee not, thou hast no part with me.*

9. *Simon Peter saith unto him, Lord, not my feet only, but also my hands and my head.*

"And supper being ended:" The Greek text is "When supper was come" or "had begun." According to the Talmud, the Pharisaic reckoning for eating the Passover was on the night of the 13th. The Sadducees kept the Passover the following night.[23] Therefore it did not arouse any suspicion or attract any undue attention when Jesus with His disciples partook of the Passover *one day ahead* of the time prescribed for the *legal* observance.

"The three synoptists [Matthew, Mark, Luke] unite in describing this solemn meal, for which Peter and John were sent to prepare, as the ordinary Paschal Supper. But, on comparing the record of the same Supper given by St. John, we are irresistibly led to a different conclusion; for we read that on the following day those who led Jesus into the Praetorium, went not in themselves, "lest they should be defiled; but that they might eat the Passover" (John 18:28). So the time of the Supper is described by John (13:1) as 'before the Feast of the Passover'."[24]

"'Messiah our Passover is sacrificed for us.' The Apostle regarded not the Last Supper, but the death of Messiah, as the antitype of the Paschal sacrifice, and the correspondence of type

---

[23]*J. Hosh.* ii. 1;10b.

[24]Spence and Exell, *The Pulpit Commentary.*

and antitype would be incomplete unless the sacrifice of the Redeemer took place at the time on which alone that of the Paschal lamb could legally be offered."[25]

"Before I suffer." "Messiah foresaw that He would have to leave His disciples before the Jewish Passover, and determined to give a peculiar meaning to His last meal with them, and to place it in a peculiar relation to the passover of the old covenant, the place of which was to be taken by the meal of the new covenant."[26]

"The simple supposition that a custom prevailed among the Jews of spreading the allowable opportunity of the sacrifice of the paschal lamb over a larger portion of time, in consequence of the great crowd in Jerusalem at the time, would really cover every difficulty, if we add to it that our Lord 'desiring to eat the passover with His disciples *before He suffered,*' had chosen to select such portions of the ritual, and such hour of the day, as best suited His dread foreknowledge of the immediate future."[27]

**TO MOUNT OF OLIVES AFTER SUPPER**

### *Matthew 26:30, 36-46*

30. *And when they had sung an hymn, they went out into the mount of Olives.*
36. *Then cometh Jesus with them unto a place called Gethsemane*[28], *and saith unto the disciples, Sit ye here, while I go and pray yonder.*
37. *And he took with him Peter and the two sons of Zebedee, and began to be sorrowful and very heavy.*

---

[25]Dean Mansel.
[26]Neander, *Life of Messiah.*
[27]Dr. Reynolds.
[28]Signifies "oil press." It was an olive yard lying at the western feet of Olivet, on the way to Bethany.

38. *Then saith he unto them, My soul is exceeding sorrowful, even unto death: tarry ye here, and watch with me.*

39. *And he went a little farther, and fell on his face, and prayed, saying, O my Father, if it be possible, let this cup pass from me: nevertheless not as I will, but as thou wilt.*

40. *And he cometh unto the disciples, and findeth them asleep, and saith unto Peter, What, could ye not watch with me one hour?*

41. *Watch and pray, that ye enter not into temptation: the spirit indeed is willing, but the flesh is weak.*

42. *He went away again the second time, and prayed, saying, O my Father, if this cup may not pass away from me, except I drink it, thy will be done.*

43. *And he came and found them asleep again: for their eyes were heavy.*

44. *And he left them, and went away again, and prayed the third time, saying the same words.*

45. *Then cometh he to his disciples, and saith unto them, Sleep on now, and take your rest: behold, the hour is at hand, and the Son of man is betrayed into the hands of sinners.*

46. *Rise, let us be going: behold, he is at hand that doth betray me.*

### Mark 14:26, 32-38

26. *And when they had sung an hymn\*, they went out into the mount of Olives.*

32. *And they came to a place which was named Gethsemane: and he saith to his disciples, Sit ye here, while I shall pray.*

33. *And he taketh with him Peter and James and John, and began to be sore amazed, and to be very heavy;*

\*The Hymn they sang is called "Hallel" meaning "Praise," Psalms 113 through 118. Jewish people still chant this Hymn at their Passover celebration. It is certainly striking that at the very time the Jews were singing or chanting the Hallel, the praises to God, they were fulfilling those very Scriptures (see Psalm 118:22)!

34. And saith unto them, My soul is exceeding sorrowful unto death: tarry ye here, and watch.

35. And he went forward a little, and fell on the ground, and prayed that, if it were possible, the hour might pass from him.

36. And he said, Abba[29], Father[30], all things are possible unto thee; take away this cup from me: nevertheless not what I will, but what thou wilt.

37. And he cometh, and findeth them sleeping, and saith unto Peter, Simon, sleepest thou? couldest not thou watch one hour?

38. And he cometh, and findeth them sleeping, and saith unto Peter, Simon, sleepest thou? couldest not thou watch one hour?

### Mark 14:39-42

39. And again he went away, and prayed, and spake the same words.

40. And when he returned, he found them asleep again, (for their eyes were heavy,) neither wist they what to answer him.

41. And he cometh the third time, and saith unto them, Sleep on now, and take your rest: it is enough, the hour is come; behold, the Son of man is betrayed into the hands of sinners.

42. Rise up, let us go; lo, he that betrayeth me is at hand.

### Luke 22:39-46

39. And he came out, and went, as he was wont, to the mount of Olives; and his disciples also followed him.

40. And when he was at the place, he said unto them, Pray that ye enter not into temptation.

41. And he was withdrawn from them about a stone's cast, and kneeled down, and prayed,

42. Saying, Father, if thou be willing, remove this cup from me: nevertheless not my will, but thine, be done.

---

[29]This is an Aramaic term for "Father."
[30]The Greek word is *pater*.

43. And there appeared an angel unto him from heaven, strengthening him.

44. And being in an agony he prayed more earnestly: and his sweat was as it were great drops of blood falling down to the ground.

45. And when he rose up from prayer, and was come to his disciples, he found them sleeping for sorrow,

46. And said unto them, Why sleep ye? rise and pray, lest ye enter into temptation.

### John 18:1

1. When Jesus had spoken these words, he went forth with his disciples over the brook Cedron, where was a garden, into the which he entered, and his disciples.

**BETRAYAL AND ARREST** (This took place around midnight.)

### Matthew 26:47-56

47. And while he yet spake, lo, Judas, one of the twelve, came, and with him a great multitude with swords and staves, from the chief priests and elders of the people.

48. Now he that betrayed him gave them a sign, saying, Whomsoever I shall kiss, that same is he: hold him fast.

49. And forthwith he came to Jesus, and said, Hail, master; and kissed him.

50. And Jesus said unto him, Friend, wherefore art thou come? Then came they, and laid hands on Jesus, and took him.

51. And, behold, one of them which were with Jesus stretched out his hand, and drew his sword, and struck a servant of the high priest's, and smote off his ear.

52. Then said Jesus unto him, Put up again thy sword into his place: for all they that take the sword shall perish with the sword.

53. Thinkest thou that I cannot now pray to my Father, and he shall presently give me more than twelve legions of angels?

54. *But how then shall the scriptures be fulfilled, that thus it must be?*

55. *In that same hour said Jesus to the multitudes, Are ye come out as against a thief with swords and staves for to take me? I sat daily with you teaching in the temple, and ye laid no hold on me.*

56. *But all this was done, that the scriptures of the prophets might be fulfilled. Then all the disciples forsook him, and fled.*

### Mark 14:43-52

43. *And immediately, while he yet spake, cometh Judas, one of the twelve, and with him a great multitude with swords and staves, from the chief priests and the scribes and the elders.*

44. *And he that betrayed him had given them a token, saying, Whomsoever I shall kiss, that same is he; take him, and lead him away safely.*

45. *And as soon as he was come, he goeth straightway to him, and saith, Master, master; and kissed him.*

46. *And they laid their hands on him, and took him.*

47. *And one of them that stood by drew a sword, and smote a servant of the high priest, and cut off his ear.*

48. *And Jesus answered and said unto them, Are ye come out, as against a thief, with swords and with staves to take me?*

49. *I was daily with you in the temple teaching, and ye took me not: but the scriptures must be fulfilled.*

50. *And they all forsook him, and fled.*

51. *And there followed him a certain young man, having a linen cloth cast about his naked body; and the young men laid hold on him:*

52. *And he left the linen cloth, and fled from them naked.*

Messiah Yeshua repeatedly emphasized that the Scriptures must be fulfilled. He was to be betrayed by His "familiar friend," He would not fight against those who came to take Him to judgment and trial, and "all would forsake Him." This was all prophesied in the T'nakh (OT)!

## Luke 22:47-53

47. And while he yet spake, behold a multitude, and he that was called Judas, one of the twelve, went before them, and drew near unto Jesus to kiss him.

48. But Jesus said unto him, Judas, betrayest thou the Son of man with a kiss?

49. When they which were about him saw what would follow, they said unto him, Lord, shall we smite with the sword?

50. And one of them smote the servant of the high priest, and cut off his right ear.

51. And Jesus answered and said, Suffer ye thus far. And he touched his ear, and healed him.

52. Then Jesus said unto the chief priests, and captains of the temple, and the elders, which were come to him, Be ye come out, as against a thief, with swords and staves?

53. When I was daily with you in the temple, ye stretched forth no hands against me: but this is your hour, and the power of darkness.

## John 18:1-11

1. When Jesus had spoken these words, he went forth with his disciples over the brook Cedron, where was a garden, into the which he entered, and his disciples.

2. And Judas also, which betrayed him, knew the place: for Jesus ofttimes resorted thither with his disciples.

3. Judas then, having received a band of men and officers from the chief priests and Pharisees, cometh thither with lanterns and torches and weapons.

4. Jesus therefore, knowing all things that should come upon him, went forth, and said unto them, Whom seek ye?

5. They answered him, Jesus of Nazareth. Jesus saith unto them, I am he. And Judas also, which betrayed him, stood with them.

6. As soon then as he had said unto them, I am he, they went backward, and fell to the ground.

7.   Then asked he them again, Whom seek ye? And they said, Jesus of Nazareth.

8.   Jesus answered, I have told you that I am he: if therefore ye seek me, let these go their way:

9.   That the saying might be fulfilled, which he spake, Of them which thou gavest me have I lost none.

10.   Then Simon Peter having a sword drew it, and smote the high priest's servant, and cut off his right ear. The servant's name was Malchus.

11.   Then said Jesus unto Peter, Put up thy sword into the sheath: the cup which my Father hath given me, shall I not drink it?

**THE TRIAL BEFORE JEWISH AUTHORITIES**

## Matthew 26:57-69

57.   And they that had laid hold on Jesus led him away to Caiaphas the high priest, where the scribes and the elders were assembled.

58.   But Peter followed him afar off unto the high priest's palace, and went in, and sat with the servants, to see the end.

59.   Now the chief priests, and elders, and all the council, sought false witness against Jesus, to put him to death;

60.   But found none: yea, though many false witnesses came, yet found they none. At the last came two false witnesses,

61.   And said, This fellow said, I am able to destroy the temple of God, and to build it in three days.

62.   And the high priest arose, and said unto him, Answerest thou nothing? what is it which these witness against thee?

63.   But Jesus held his peace. And the high priest answered and said unto him, I adjure thee by the living God, that thou tell us whether thou be the Christ, the Son of God.

64.   Jesus saith unto him, Thou hast said: nevertheless I say unto you, Hereafter shall ye see the Son of man sitting on the right hand of power, and coming in the clouds of heaven.

65. *Then the high priest rent his clothes, saying, He hath spoken blasphemy; what further need have we of witnesses? behold, now ye have heard his blasphemy.*

66. *What think ye? They answered and said, He is guilty of death.*

67. *Then did they spit in his face, and buffeted him; and others smote him with the palms of their hands,*

68. *Saying, Prophesy unto us, thou Christ, Who is he that smote thee?*

69. *Now Peter sat without in the palace: and a damsel came unto him, saying, Thou also wast with Jesus of Galilee.*

### *Matthew 27:1*

1. *When the morning was come, all the chief priests and elders of the people took counsel against Jesus to put him to death:*

### *Mark 14:53-65*

53. *And they led Jesus away to the high priest: and with him were assembled all the chief priests and the elders and the scribes.*

54. *And Peter followed him afar off, even into the palace of the high priest: and he sat with the servants, and warmed himself at the fire.*

55. *And the chief priests and all the council sought for witness against Jesus to put him to death; and found none.*

56. *For many bare false witness against him, but their witness agreed not together.*

57. *And there arose certain, and bare false witness against him, saying,*

58. *We heard him say, I will destroy this temple that is made with hands, and within three days I will build another made without hands.*

59. *But neither so did their witness agree together.*

60. *And the high priest stood up in the midst, and asked Jesus, saying, Answerest thou nothing? what is it which these witness against thee?*

61. *But he held his peace, and answered nothing. Again the high priest asked him, and said unto him, Art thou the Christ, the Son of the Blessed?*

62. *And Jesus said, I am: and ye shall see the Son of man sitting on the right hand of power, and coming in the clouds of heaven.*

63. *Then the high priest rent his clothes, and saith, What need we any further witnesses?*

64. *Ye have heard the blasphemy: what think ye? And they all condemned him to be guilty of death.*

65. *And some began to spit on him, and to cover his face, and to buffet him, and to say unto him, Prophesy: and the servants did strike him with the palms of their hands.*

### Luke 22:54, 63-71

54. *Then took they him, and led him, and brought him into the high priest's house. And Peter followed afar off.*

63. *And the men that held Jesus mocked him, and smote him.*

64. *And when they had blindfolded him, they struck him on the face, and asked him, saying, Prophesy, who is it that smote thee?*

65. *And many other things blasphemously spake they against him.*

66. *And as soon as **it was day**, the elders of the people and the chief priests and the scribes came together, and led him into their council, saying,*

67. *Art thou the Christ? tell us. And he said unto them, If I tell you, ye will not believe:*

68. *And if I also ask you, ye will not answer me, nor let me go.*

69. *Hereafter shall the Son of man sit on the right hand of the power of God.*

70. *Then said they all, Art thou then the Son of God? And he said unto them, Ye say that I am.*

71. *And they said, What need we any further witness? for we ourselves have heard of his own mouth.*

The first Jewish trial lasted until morning and was *illegal* because it was held at night. Now, to legalize the proceedings, Jesus is further tried before Jewish officials as a mere formality which would be over in a few minutes. According to the Pharisaic law it was not lawful for the Sanhedrin, either the Greater or the Lesser Sanhedrin, to sit on the eve of the Sabbath or on the eve of or during a festival.[31]

---

[31]See *Mishnah, Sanh.* IV.1.

# A JUDGE LOOKS AT
# THE TRIAL OF JESUS

by The Honorable Wyatt H. Heard

Judge, 190th Judicial District Court

Harris County, Texas

The *arrest* of Jesus in Gethsemane was illegal [*The Bab. Talmud: Sanhedrin I,* ch. IV, *Mishna,*] because:
- The arrest took place at night in violation of Hebrew law.
- The arrest was effected through the agency of a traitor and informer in violation of the Mosaic code of Leviticus 19:16-18.
- It was not the result of a legal mandate from a court whose intention was to conduct a legal trial.

The *private examination* of Jesus before the High Priest was illegal because:
- The examination was conducted at night in violation of Hebrew law *(ibid)*.
- No judge sitting alone could interrogate an accused judicially or sit in judgment upon his legal rights *(ibid; Deuteronomy 19:16-18)*.
- Private preliminary examination of an accused was not allowed by the Hebrew law *(ibid)*.

The *indictment* against Jesus was in form illegal because:
- The accusation at the trial was twofold, vague, and indefinite, which Mosaic law forbade (Deuteronomy 17:2-6; 19:15).
- It was made in part by the High Priest (Caiaphas) who was one of the judges of Jesus when in fact Hebrew law only allowed leading witnesses to present the charge (Deuteronomy 17:6).

The *proceedings* of the Sanhedrin against Jesus were illegal because:

- The court convened before the offering of the morning sacrifice *(ibid)*.
- They were conducted on: 1) the day preceding a Jewish Sabbath; 2) on the first day of the Feast of Unleavened Bread; 3) on the Eve of the Passover. "They shall not judge on the Eve of the Sabbath, nor on that of any festival" *(ibid)*.

The *trial* of Jesus was illegal because it was concluded within one day. "A criminal case resulting in the acquittal of the accused may terminate the same day on which the trial began; but if a sentence of death is to be pronounced, it cannot be concluded before the following day" *(ibid)*.

The *sentence* of condemnation was illegal: The sentence of condemnation pronounced against Jesus by the Sanhedrin was illegal because it was founded upon his uncorroborated confession. (Mendelsohn: *Criminal Jurisprudence of the Ancient Hebrews,* p. 133; Maimonides: *Sanhedrin,* Ch. IV, 2).

The *condemnation* was illegal: The condemnation of Jesus was illegal because the verdict of the Sanhedrin was unanimous. "A simultaneous and unanimous verdict of guilty rendered on the day of the trial has the effect of an acquittal" (Mendelsohn, *opus cit.,* p. 141; Mark 14:64).

The *proceedings* against Jesus were illegal in that the sentence of condemnation was pronounced in a place forbidden by law: "Any sentence of death or trial must be held in the Hall of Hewn Stones" (Talmud).

The *Sanhedrin* legally disqualified: The members of the great Sanhedrin were legally disqualified to try Jesus. "No judge could sit in Judgment if he be at enmity with the accused person or he had formed a preconceived idea concerning him" (Mendelsohn: *Hebrew Maxims and Rules*).

We recognize that the scribes and Pharisees were provoked by Jesus long before his trial; that Caiaphas the High Priest had said: " … It is expedient for us, that one man should die for the people, and that the whole nation perish not … From that day forth they took counsel together for to put him to death" [John 11:50-53].

–Reprinted from *Psychology for Living,* Narramore Christian Foundation, Rosemead, California. (Also see Appendix IV: *Jesus Before the Bar.*)

## *John 18:12-14, 19-24*

12. Then the band and the captain and officers of the Jews took Jesus, and bound him,

13. And led him away to Annas first; for he was father in law to Caiaphas, which was the high priest that same year.

14. Now Caiaphas was he, which gave counsel to the Jews, that it was expedient that one man should die for the people.

19. The high priest then asked Jesus of his disciples, and of his doctrine.

20. Jesus answered him, I spake openly to the world; I ever taught in the synagogue, and in the temple, whither the Jews always resort; and in secret have I said nothing.

21. Why askest thou me? ask them which heard me, what I have said unto them: behold, they know what I said.

22. And when he had thus spoken, one of the officers which stood by struck Jesus with the palm of his hand, saying, Answerest thou the high priest so?

23. Jesus answered him, If I have spoken evil, bear witness of the evil: but if well, why smitest thou me?

24. Now Annas had sent him bound unto Caiaphas the high priest.

**PETER'S DENIALS**

## *Matthew 26:69-75*

69. Now Peter sat without in the palace: and a damsel came unto him, saying, Thou also wast with Jesus of Galilee.

70. But he denied before them all, saying, I know not what thou sayest.

71. And when he was gone out into the porch, another maid saw him, and said unto them that were there, This fellow was also with Jesus of Nazareth.

72. And again he denied with an oath, I do not know the man.

73. And after a while came unto him they that stood by, and said to Peter, Surely thou also art one of them; for thy speech bewrayeth thee.

74. *Then began he to curse and to swear, saying, I know not the man. And immediately the cock crew.*

75. *And Peter remembered the word of Jesus, which said unto him, Before the cock crow, thou shalt deny me thrice. And he went out, and wept bitterly.*

### Mark 14:66-72

66. *And as Peter was beneath in the palace, there cometh one of the maids of the high priest:*

67. *And when she saw Peter warming himself, she looked upon him, and said, And thou also wast with Jesus of Nazareth.*

68. *But he denied, saying, I know not, neither understand I what thou sayest. And he went out into the porch; and the cock crew.*

69. *And a maid saw him again, and began to say to them that stood by, This is one of them.*

70. *And he denied it again. And a little after, they that stood by said again to Peter, Surely thou art one of them: for thou art a Galilaean, and thy speech agreeth thereto.*

71. *But he began to curse and to swear, saying, I know not this man of whom ye speak.*

72. *And the second time the cock crew. And Peter called to mind the word that Jesus said unto him, Before the cock crow twice, thou shalt deny me thrice. And when he thought thereon, he wept.*

"In relating both our Lord's words and Peter's denial, Mark alone mentions a second cock-crowing (Mark 14:30). The cock often crows irregularly about midnight, or not long after; and again always, and regularly about the third hour, or daybreak. When, therefore, 'the cock-crowing' is spoken of indefinitely, this last is always meant. Hence the name 'cock-crowing' was used for the third watch of the night, which ended at the third hour after midnight (Mark 13:35). Mark, therefore, here relates more definitely; the others more generally."[32]

---

[32]Irwin's *Bible Commentary.*

*55. And when they had kindled a fire in the midst of the hall, and were set down together, Peter sat down among them.*

*56. But a certain maid beheld him as he sat by the fire, and earnestly looked upon him, and said, This man was also with him.*

*57. And he denied him, saying, Woman, I know him not.*

*58. And after a little while another saw him, and said, Thou art also of them. And Peter said, Man, I am not.*

*59. And about the space of one hour after another confidently affirmed, saying, Of a truth this fellow also was with him: for he is a Galilaean.*

*60. And Peter said, Man, I know not what thou sayest. And immediately, while he yet spake, the cock crew.*

*61. And the Lord turned, and looked upon Peter. And Peter remembered the word of the Lord, how he had said unto him, Before the cock crow, thou shalt deny me thrice.*

*62. And Peter went out, and wept bitterly.*

According to Jewish rabbis, no cocks were allowed in Jerusalem at the time of the Passover. However, the castle of Antonia, which was situated on the northwest corner of the Temple area, housed the Roman soldiers who possessed these cocks in their quarters. At each watch and at cock-crowings, the Romans relieved a guard who was on duty.

## John 18:15-18, 25-27

*15. And Simon Peter followed Jesus, and so did another disciple: that disciple was known unto the high priest, and went in with Jesus into the palace of the high priest.*

*16. But Peter stood at the door without. Then went out that other disciple, which was known unto the high priest, and spake unto her that kept the door, and brought in Peter.*

*17. Then saith the damsel that kept the door unto Peter, Art not thou also one of this man's disciples? He saith, I am not.*

18. *And the servants and officers stood there, who had made a fire of coals; for it was cold: and they warmed themselves: and Peter stood with them, and warmed himself.*

25. *And Simon Peter stood and warmed himself. They said therefore unto him, Art not thou also one of his disciples? He denied it, and said, I am not.*

26. *One of the servants of the high priest, being his kinsman whose ear Peter cut off, saith, Did not I see thee in the garden with him?*

27. *Peter then denied again: and immediately the cock crew.*

### TO PILATE-TO HEROD-AND BACK TO PILATE

### *Matthew 27:2, 11-14*

2. *And when they had bound him, they led him away, and delivered him to Pontius Pilate the governor.*

11. *And Jesus stood before the governor: and the governor asked him, saying, Art thou the King of the Jews? And Jesus said unto him, Thou sayest.*

12. *And when he was accused of the chief priests and elders, he answered nothing.*

13. *Then said Pilate unto him, Hearest thou not how many things they witness against thee?*

14. *And he answered him to never a word; insomuch that the governor marvelled greatly.*

### *Mark 15:1-5*

1. *And straightway in the morning the chief priests held a consultation with the elders and scribes and the whole council, and bound Jesus, and carried him away, and delivered him to Pilate.*

2. *And Pilate asked him, Art thou the King of the Jews? And he answering said unto him, Thou sayest it.*

3. *And the chief priests accused him of many things: but he answered nothing.*

4. And Pilate asked him again, saying, Answerest thou nothing? behold how many things they witness against thee.

5. But Jesus yet answered nothing; so that Pilate marvelled.

### Luke 23:1-16

1. And the whole multitude of them arose, and led him unto Pilate.

2. And they began to accuse him, saying, We found this fellow perverting the nation, and forbidding to give tribute to Caesar, saying that he himself is Christ a King.

3. And Pilate asked him, saying, Art thou the King of the Jews? And he answered him and said, Thou sayest it.

4. Then said Pilate to the chief priests and to the people, I find no fault in this man.

5. And they were the more fierce, saying, He stirreth up the people, teaching throughout all Jewry, beginning from Galilee to this place.

6. When Pilate heard of Galilee, he asked whether the man were a Galilaean.

7. And as soon as he knew that he belonged unto Herod's jurisdiction, he sent him to Herod, who himself also was at Jerusalem at that time.

8. And when Herod saw Jesus, he was exceeding glad: for he was desirous to see him of a long season, because he had heard many things of him; and he hoped to have seen some miracle done by him.

9. Then he questioned with him in many words; but he answered him nothing.

10. And the chief priests and scribes stood and vehemently accused him.

11. And Herod with his men of war set him at nought, and mocked him, and arrayed him in a gorgeous robe, and sent him again to Pilate.

12. And the same day Pilate and Herod were made friends together: for before they were at enmity between themselves.

*13. And Pilate, when he had called together the chief priests and the rulers and the people,*

*14. Said unto them, Ye have brought this man unto me, as one that perverteth the people: and, behold, I, having examined him before you, have found no fault in this man touching those things whereof ye accuse him:*

*15. Said unto them, Ye have brought this man unto me, as one that perverteth the people: and, behold, I, having examined him before you, have found no fault in this man touching those things whereof ye accuse him:*

*16. I will therefore chastise him, and release him.*

"The civil trial took place, first before Pilate, then before Herod, and, lastly, before Pilate again."[33]

## *John 18:28-38*

*28. Then led they Jesus from Caiaphas unto the hall of judgment: and* **it was early;** [The ecclesiastical trial before Caiaphas had taken place before daylight. Now it is between five and six in the morning, about sunrise.] *and they themselves went not into the judgment hall, lest they should be defiled; but that they might eat the passover.*

*29. Pilate then went out unto them, and said, What accusation bring ye against this man?*

*30. They answered and said unto him, If he were not a malefactor, we would not have delivered him up unto thee.*

*31. Then said Pilate unto them, Take ye him, and judge him according to your law. The Jews therefore said unto him, It is not lawful for us to put any man to death:*

*32. That the saying of Jesus might be fulfilled, which he spake, signifying what death he should die.*

*33. Then Pilate entered into the judgment hall again, and called Jesus, and said unto him, Art thou the King of the Jews?*

*34. Jesus answered him, Sayest thou this thing of thyself, or did others tell it thee of me?*

---

[33]Rev. James Stalker, M.A., *Life of Messiah.*

35. *Pilate answered, Am I a Jew? Thine own nation and the chief priests have delivered thee unto me: what hast thou done?*

36. *Jesus answered, My kingdom is not of this world: if my kingdom were of this world, then would my servants fight, that I should not be delivered to the Jews: but now is my kingdom not from hence.*

37. *Pilate therefore said unto him, Art thou a king then? Jesus answered, Thou sayest that I am a king. To this end was I born, and for this cause came I into the world, that I should bear witness unto the truth. Every one that is of the truth heareth my voice.*

38. *Pilate saith unto him, What is truth? And when he had said this, he went out again unto the Jews, and saith unto them, I find in him no fault at all.*

### *John 19:1, 4-15*

1. *Then Pilate therefore took Jesus, and scourged him.*

4. *Pilate therefore went forth again, and saith unto them, Behold, I bring him forth to you, that ye may know that I find no fault in him.*

5. *Then came Jesus forth, wearing the crown of thorns, and the purple robe. And Pilate saith unto them, Behold the man!*

6. *When the chief priests therefore and officers saw him, they cried out, saying, Crucify him, crucify him. Pilate saith unto them, Take ye him, and crucify him: for I find no fault in him.*

7. *The Jews answered him, We have a law, and by our law he ought to die, because he made himself the Son of God.*

8. *When Pilate therefore heard that saying, he was the more afraid;*

9. *And went again into the judgment hall, and saith unto Jesus, Whence art thou? But Jesus gave him no answer.*

10. *Then saith Pilate unto him, Speakest thou not unto me? knowest thou not that I have power to crucify thee, and have power to release thee?*

11. *Jesus answered, Thou couldest have no power at all against me, except it were given thee from above: therefore he that delivered me unto thee hath the greater sin.*

12. *And from thenceforth Pilate sought to release him: but the Jews cried out, saying, If thou let this man go, thou art not Caesar's friend: whosoever maketh himself a king speaketh against Caesar.*

13. *When Pilate therefore heard that saying, he brought Jesus forth, and sat down in the judgment seat in a place that is called the Pavement, but in the Hebrew, Gabbatha.*

14. *And it was the **preparation of the passover,** and about the **sixth hour**: and he saith unto the Jews, Behold your King!*

15. *But they cried out, Away with him, away with him, crucify him. Pilate saith unto them, Shall I crucify your King? The chief priests answered, We have no king but Caesar.*

John wrote this Gospel in Asia Minor late in the century long after the destruction of Jerusalem when the Jewish method of acknowledging time would not likely be preserved. He evidently is not writing for the Jews primarily, since he constantly speaks of them as outsiders. Therefore John makes the day begin at midnight as the Romans did, for Roman ideas were prevalent in Asia Minor. Here then we understand that Pilate passed the sentence at *six o'clock.*

### John's Reckoning of Time

We find examples of John's reckoning of time in the following:

"'It was about the tenth hour' (John 1:39). It was the way of the ancients to divide the day into twelve hours, and the night into as many. The first hour of the day was an hour after the sun rose, and the twelfth was when it set. This was the way in Judea, and to this the other Evangelists adhere. But John appears to have reckoned the hours as we do, from midnight to noon, and again from noon to midnight. And it may be observed, that he mentions the hour of the day oftener than any other evangelist; as if with design to give his readers an opportunity of discerning this method, by comparing one passage with another. If the time here intended was that which we may call Jewish (to distinguish it, not from the Greek and Roman which were the same with the Jewish, but from the modern); the tenth hour was about four in the afternoon, or two hours before the day ended in Judea, with which time neither the words nor circumstances of the narration seem to agree. For the words, *they abode with him that day*, rather imply that they spent a good part of the day with him. Therefore the most reasonable account of this tenth hour is, that it was ten in the morning. And in John 4:6, we have another example: According to John's computation of time, this would be six o'clock in the afternoon. The women of the East have stated times for going to draw water–not in the heat of the day, but in the cool of either morning or evening. It was very likely in the evening that this Samaritan woman came to draw water, because it is said, Jesus had become weary with his journey; and because the Samaritans when they came to see him, invited him to remain and lodge with them."[34]

## BARABBAS OR JESUS

### *Matthew 27:15-26*

15. *Now at that feast the governor was wont to release unto the people a prisoner, whom they would.*

16. *And they had then a notable prisoner, called Barabbas.*

17. *Therefore when they were gathered together, Pilate said unto them, Whom will ye that I release unto you? Barabbas, or Jesus which is called Christ?*

18. *For he knew that for envy they had delivered him.*

19. *When he was set down on the judgment seat, his wife sent unto him, saying, Have thou nothing to do with that just man: for I have suffered many things this day in a dream because of him.*

20. *But the chief priests and elders persuaded the multitude that they should ask Barabbas, and destroy Jesus.*

21. *The governor answered and said unto them, Whether of the twain will ye that I release unto you? They said, Barabbas.*

---

[34]Townson, *Discourses on the Four Gospels.*

22. *Pilate saith unto them, What shall I do then with Jesus which is called Christ? They all say unto him, Let him be crucified.*

23. *And the governor said, Why, what evil hath he done? But they cried out the more, saying, Let him be crucified.*

24. *When Pilate saw that he could prevail nothing, but that rather a tumult was made, he took water, and washed his hands before the multitude, saying, I am innocent of the blood of this just person: see ye to it.*

25. *Then answered all the people, and said, His blood be on us, and on our children.*

26. *Then released he Barabbas unto them: and when he had scourged Jesus, he delivered him to be crucified.*

### *Mark 15:6-15*

6. *Now at **that** feast [Passover] he released unto them one prisoner, whomsoever they desired.*

7. *And there was one named Barabbas, which lay bound with them that had made insurrection with him, who had committed murder in the insurrection.*

8. *And the multitude crying aloud began to desire him to do as he had ever done unto them.*

9. *But Pilate answered them, saying, Will ye that I release unto you the King of the Jews?*

10. *For he knew that the chief priests had delivered him for envy.*

11. *But the chief priests moved the people, that he should rather release Barabbas unto them.*

12. *And Pilate answered and said again unto them, What will ye then that I shall do unto him whom ye call the King of the Jews?*

13. *And they cried out again, Crucify him.*

14. *Then Pilate said unto them, Why, what evil hath he done? And they cried out the more exceedingly, Crucify him.*

15. *And so Pilate, willing to content the people, released Barabbas unto them, and delivered Jesus, when he had scourged him, to be crucified.*

17. *(For of necessity he must release one unto them at the feast.)*[35]
18. *And they cried out all at once, saying, Away with this man, and release unto us Barabbas:*
19. *(Who for a certain sedition made in the city, and for murder, was cast into prison.)*
20. *Pilate therefore, willing to release Jesus, spake again to them.*
21. *But they cried, saying, Crucify him, crucify him.*
22. *And he said unto them the third time, Why, what evil hath he done? I have found no cause of death in him: I will therefore chastise him, and let him go.*
23. *And they were instant with loud voices, requiring that he might be crucified. And the voices of them and of the chief priests prevailed.*
24. *And Pilate gave sentence that it should be as they required.*
25. *And he released unto them him that for sedition and murder was cast into prison, whom they had desired; but he delivered Jesus to their will.*

### *John 18:39-40*

39. *But ye have a custom, that I should release unto you one at the passover: will ye therefore that I release unto you the King of the Jews?*
40. *Then cried they all again, saying, Not this man, but Barabbas. Now Barabbas was a robber.*

**MOCKING AND SCOURGING BY ROMAN SOLDIERS**

### *Matthew 27:27-31*

27. *Then the soldiers of the governor took Jesus into the common hall, and gathered unto him the whole band of soldiers.*

---

[35]See John 18:39. It was the custom to release a prisoner at the Passover in remembrance of Israel's deliverance from slavery in Egypt at that *first* Passover.

28. *And they stripped him, and put on him a scarlet robe.*

29. *And when they had platted a crown of thorns, they put it upon his head, and a reed in his right hand: and they bowed the knee before him, and mocked him, saying, Hail, King of the Jews!*

30. *And they spit upon him, and took the reed, and smote him on the head.*

31. *And after that they had mocked him, they took the robe off from him, and put his own raiment on him, and led him away to crucify him.*

### Mark 15:16-20

16. *And the soldiers led him away into the hall, called Praetorium; and they call together the whole band.*

17. *And they clothed him with purple, and platted a crown of thorns, and put it about his head,*

18. *And began to salute him, Hail, King of the Jews!*

19. *And they smote him on the head with a reed, and did spit upon him, and bowing their knees worshipped him.*

20. *And when they had mocked him, they took off the purple from him, and put his own clothes on him, and led him out to crucify him.*

### Luke 23:11

11. *And Herod with his men of war set him at nought, and mocked him, and arrayed him in a gorgeous robe, and sent him again to Pilate.*

### John 19:2-3

2. *And the soldiers platted a crown of thorns, and put it on his head, and they put on him a purple robe,*

3. *And said, Hail, King of the Jews! and they smote him with their hands.*

## *Matthew 27:3-10*

3. *Then Judas, which had betrayed him, when he saw that he was condemned, repented himself, and brought again the thirty pieces of silver to the chief priests and elders,*
4. *Saying, I have sinned in that I have betrayed the innocent blood. And they said, What is that to us? see thou to that.*
5. *And he cast down the pieces of silver in the temple, and departed, and went and hanged himself.*
6. *And the chief priests took the silver pieces, and said, It is not lawful for to put them into the treasury, because it is the price of blood.*
7. *And they took counsel, and bought with them the potter's field, to bury strangers in.*
8. *Wherefore that field was called, The field of blood, unto this day.*
9. *Then was fulfilled that which was spoken by Jeremy the prophet, saying, And they took the thirty pieces of silver, the price of him that was valued, whom they of the children of Israel did value;*
10. *And gave them for the potter's field, as the Lord appointed me.*

### THE CRUCIFIXION

The *night* of Nisan 14 was all used in trying, testing, examining the Lamb for the last time before offering Him on the altar of sacrifice. Upon the people of Israel as well as upon the Gentile world the night of sin had settled. They fulfilled God's Word and plan even in the darkness of their minds and hearts!

32. And as they came out, they found a man of Cyrene, Simon by name: him they compelled to bear his cross.

33. And when they were come unto a place called Golgotha, that is to say, a place of a skull,

34. They gave him vinegar to drink mingled with gall: and when he had tasted thereof, he would not drink.

35. And they **crucified** him, and parted his garments, casting lots: that it might be fulfilled which was spoken by the prophet, They parted my garments among them, and upon my vesture did they cast lots.[36]

36. And sitting down they watched him there;

37. And set up over his head his accusation written, THIS IS JESUS THE KING OF THE JEWS.

38. Then were there two thieves crucified with him, one on the right hand, and another on the left.

39. And they that passed by reviled him, wagging their heads,

40. And saying, Thou that destroyest the temple, and buildest it in three days, save thyself. If thou be the Son of God, come down from the cross.

41. Likewise also the chief priests mocking him, with the scribes and elders, said,

42. He saved others; himself he cannot save. If he be the King of Israel, let him now come down from the cross, and we will believe him.

43. He trusted in God; let him deliver him now, if he will have him: for he said, I am the Son of God.

44. The thieves also, which were crucified with him, cast the same in his teeth.

45. Now from the sixth hour there was darkness over all the land unto the ninth hour.

46. And about **the ninth hour** [three o'clock in the afternoon] Jesus cried with a loud voice, saying, Eli, Eli, lama

---

[36]See Psalm 22:18.

*sabachthani? that is to say, My God, my God, why hast thou forsaken me?*

47. *Some of them that stood there, when they heard that, said, This man calleth for Elias.*

48. *And straightway one of them ran, and took a sponge, and filled it with vinegar, and put it on a reed, and gave him to drink.*

49. *The rest said, Let be, let us see whether Elias will come to save him.*

50. *Jesus, when he had cried again with a loud voice, yielded up the ghost.*

51. *And, behold, the veil of the temple was rent in twain from the top to the bottom; and the earth did quake, and the rocks rent;*

52. *And the graves were opened; and many bodies of the saints which slept arose,*

53. *And came out of the graves after his resurrection, and went into the holy city, and appeared unto many.*

54. *Now when the centurion, and they that were with him, watching Jesus, saw the earthquake, and those things that were done, they feared greatly, saying, Truly this was the Son of God.*

55. *And many women were there beholding afar off, which followed Jesus from Galilee, ministering unto him:*

56. *Among which was Mary Magdalene, and Mary the mother of James and Joses, and the mother of Zebedee's children.*

### Mark 15:21-25

21. *And they compel one Simon a Cyrenian, who passed by, coming out of the country, the father of Alexander and Rufus, to bear his cross.*

22. *And they bring him unto the place Golgotha, which is, being interpreted, The place of a skull.*

23. *And they gave him to drink wine mingled with myrrh: but he received it not.*

*24. And when they had crucified him, they parted his garments, casting lots upon them, what every man should take.*

*25. And it was **the third hour**, and they crucified him.*

"The third hour" = nine o'clock in the morning. This means the hour when He was **nailed** to the cross ("… and they crucified him"). He was alive until the ninth hour (3 p.m.) which was the time of His **death**, i.e., when He cried with a loud voice (v. 34).

The Old Testament Scriptures inform us of God's commandment to the Children of Israel to offer a lamb as a burnt offering *in the morning* (the morning lamb), as well as another burnt offering at *three o'clock in the afternoon* (the evening lamb). See Exodus 29:39 and Numbers 28:4. Messiah was the Lamb offered at 9 a.m. (Mark 15:25) and the Lamb offered at 3 p.m. (Matthew 27:46) according to the prophecy!

### Mark 15:26-34

*26. And the superscription of his accusation was written over, THE KING OF THE JEWS.*

*27. And with him they crucify two thieves; the one on his right hand, and the other on his left.*

*28. And the scripture was fulfilled, which saith, And he was numbered with the transgressors.*

*29. And they that passed by railed on him, wagging their heads, and saying, Ah, thou that destroyest the temple, and buildest it in three days,*

*30. Save thyself, and come down from the cross.*

*31. Likewise also the chief priests mocking said among themselves with the scribes, He saved others; himself he cannot save.*

*32. Let Christ the King of Israel descend now from the cross, that we may see and believe. And they that were crucified with him reviled him.*

*33. And when the **sixth hour** was come, there was darkness over the whole land until the **ninth hour**.*

*34. And at the **ninth hour** Jesus cried with a loud voice, saying, Eloi, Eloi, lama sabachthani? which is, being interpreted, My God, my God, why hast thou forsaken me?*

Mark 15:33. The *sixth hour* = noon, *ninth hour* = 3 p.m.

*"And ye shall keep it up until the fourteenth day of the same month: and the whole assembly of the congregation of Israel shall kill it **in the evening**"* (Exodus 12:6).

The Lord had commanded the Israelites that on Nisan 14, after the lamb had been examined and declared without spot and blemish, it was to be roasted with fire *in the evening* (Hebrew text is "between the two evenings," our three o'clock in the afternoon). The Jews believed that there were two evenings, the evening of the day, and the evening of the night. The first evening began at noon. One writer, on the words "between the two evenings," explains from the Hebrew: "We mean by this expression, the dark part of the day, after the noon hour."

Rashi[37], the great Jewish teacher, stated: "One evening began at twelve o'clock noon, and the other began at six in the evening. The six hours between these two points of time were called *'bain-ha-arbayim'* or 'between the two evenings.' But the word rendered *between* is of itself a significant word. It would indicate that the lamb would be killed between the time of the first evening and the time of the second evening. What would be the hour between the two evenings, between the first evening and the second evening? In other words, what would be the hour

---

[37]"The word RaSHI represents the name of Rabbi Solomon Yitschoki, 1040-1105, the most distinguished commentator on the Bible and Talmud. His works and his name have become synonymous in Jewish learning. Rashi's contribution to Jewish scholarship was considered so significant that when the printing press was invented, his commentary was printed even before the Bible." Abraham Mayer Heller, *The Vocabulary of Jewish Life,* pp. 204-205).

which would come just between twelve noon, and six in the evening? The answer is three o'clock." And Josephus mentions the fact that the paschal lambs were slain from the ninth to the eleventh hours; the time they began to kill them was *three o'clock.*[38]

On Nisan 14 when the Jews were roasting their lambs for the Passover ritual at *three o'clock* in the afternoon according to the law, Messiah, the Lamb of God, expired. This time of day was designated as the beginning of the "going down of the sun" (Deuteronomy 16:5-6) and the prescribed moment for starting the killing of the Passover lambs. It is the moment when the Son of man went into the heart of the earth and the *three days and three nights* of Matthew 12:40 begin to be fulfilled.

### *Mark 15:35-41*

35. *And some of them that stood by, when they heard it, said, Behold, he calleth Elias.*
36. *And one ran and filled a sponge full of vinegar, and put it on a reed, and gave him to drink, saying, Let alone; let us see whether Elias will come to take him down.*
37. *And Jesus cried with a loud voice, and gave up the ghost.*
38. *And the veil of the temple was rent in twain from the top to the bottom.*
39. *And when the centurion, which stood over against him, saw that he so cried out, and gave up the ghost, he said, Truly this man was the Son of God.*
40. *There were also women looking on afar off: among whom was Mary Magdalene, and Mary the mother of James the less and of Joses, and Salome;*
41. *(Who also, when he was in Galilee, followed him, and ministered unto him;) and many other women which came up with him unto Jerusalem.*

---

[38]See Josephus, *Jewish Wars,* chapter six, paragraph three.

26. *And as they led him away, they laid hold upon one Simon, a Cyrenian, coming out of the country, and on him they laid the cross, that he might bear it after Jesus.*

27. *And there followed him a great company of people, and of women, which also bewailed and lamented him.*

28. *But Jesus turning unto them said, Daughters of Jerusalem, weep not for me, but weep for yourselves, and for your children.*

29. *For, behold, the days are coming, in the which they shall say, Blessed are the barren, and the wombs that never bare, and the paps which never gave suck.*

30. *Then shall they begin to say to the mountains, Fall on us; and to the hills, Cover us.*

31. *For if they do these things in a green tree, what shall be done in the dry?*

32. *And there were also two other, malefactors, led with him to be put to death.*

33. *And when they were come to the place, which is called Calvary, there they crucified him, and the malefactors, one on the right hand, and the other on the left.*

34. *Then said Jesus, Father, forgive them; for they know not what they do. And they parted his raiment, and cast lots.*

35. *And the people stood beholding. And the rulers also with them derided him, saying, He saved others; let him save himself, if he be Christ, the chosen of God.*

36. *And the soldiers also mocked him, coming to him, and offering him vinegar,*

37. *And saying, If thou be the king of the Jews, save thyself.*

38. *And a superscription also was written over him in letters of **Greek** [the language of culture], and **Latin** [the language of government], and **Hebrew** [the language of religion], THIS IS THE KING OF THE JEWS.*

39. *And one of the malefactors which were hanged railed on him, saying, If thou be Christ, save thyself and us.*

63

40. *But the other answering rebuked him, saying, Dost not thou fear God, seeing thou art in the same condemnation?*

41. *And we indeed justly; for we receive the due reward of our deeds: but this man hath done nothing amiss.*

42. *And he said unto Jesus, Lord, remember me when thou comest into thy kingdom.*

43. *And Jesus said unto him, Verily I say unto thee, To day shalt thou be with me in paradise.*

44. *And it was about **the sixth hour**, and there was a darkness over all the earth until **the ninth hour**.*

45. *And the sun was darkened, and the veil of the temple was rent in the midst.*

46. *And when Jesus had cried with a loud voice, he said, Father, into thy hands I commend my spirit: and having said thus, he gave up the ghost.*

47. *Now when the centurion saw what was done, he glorified God, saying, Certainly this was a righteous man.*

48. *And all the people that came together to that sight, beholding the things which were done, smote their breasts, and returned.*

49. *And all his acquaintance, and the women that followed him from Galilee, stood afar off, beholding these things.*

### *John 19:16-31*

16. *Then delivered he him therefore unto them to be crucified. And they took Jesus, and led him away.*

17. *And he bearing his cross went forth into a place called the place of a skull, which is called in the Hebrew Golgotha:*

18. *Where they crucified him, and two others with him, on either side one, and Jesus in the midst.*

19. *And Pilate wrote a title, and put it on the cross. And the writing was, JESUS OF NAZARETH THE KING OF THE JEWS.*

20. *This title then read many of the Jews: for the place where Jesus was crucified was nigh to the city: and it was written in **Hebrew**, and **Greek**, and **Latin**.*

21. *Then said the chief priests of the Jews to Pilate, Write not, The King of the Jews; but that he said, I am King of the Jews.*

22. *Pilate answered, What I have written I have written.*

23. *Then the soldiers, when they had crucified Jesus, took his garments, and made four parts, to every soldier a part; and also his coat: now the coat was without seam, woven from the top throughout.*

24. *They said therefore among themselves, Let us not rend it, but cast lots for it, whose it shall be:* **that the scripture might be fulfilled**, *which saith, They parted my raiment among them, and for my vesture they did cast lots. These things therefore the soldiers did.*

25. *Now there stood by the cross of Jesus his mother, and his mother's sister, Mary the wife of Cleophas, and Mary Magdalene.*

26. *When Jesus therefore saw his mother, and the disciple standing by, whom he loved, he saith unto his mother, Woman, behold thy son!*

27. *Then saith he to the disciple, Behold thy mother! And from that hour that disciple took her unto his own home.*

28. *After this, Jesus knowing that all things were now accomplished,* **that the scripture might be fulfilled**, *saith, I thirst.*

29. *Now there was set a vessel full of vinegar: and they filled a sponge with vinegar, and put it upon hyssop, and put it to his mouth.*

30. *When Jesus therefore had received the vinegar, he said, It is finished: and he bowed his head, and gave up the ghost.*

31. *The Jews therefore, because it was* **the preparation,** *that the bodies should not remain upon the cross on* **the sabbath day,** *(for* **that sabbath day was an high day,**) *besought Pilate that their legs might be broken, and that they might be taken away.*

"The preparation day," "the day of the preparation," "the Jews' preparation," and "the preparation" are terms used to indicate work and arrangements for the seventh-day Sabbath. This particular preparation day *always* fell on Friday, *never* on any other day. Among orthodox Jews at present, this is still true. It is interesting to note also that the term "preparation" has been the regular name for *Friday* in the Greek language, caused by

New Testament usage! It is so in the modern Greek today. If preparations were being made for any other holy day, *that holiday would be named*, such as we find in the following Scripture, for example: "And it was the preparation *of the passover*" (John 19:14).

"In the Apocrypha (Judith 8:6) there is a name for Friday which is translated 'the eve of the Sabbath': so in Mark 15:42 'the day before the Sabbath.' This day is also called the *Preparation* (Matthew 27:62, Mark 15:42, Luke 23:54, John 19:31)."[39]

### "An High Day"

The Paschal lamb was to be *eaten* the night of Nisan 14, which was really the beginning of a new day, the 15th of Nisan, or the Feast of Unleavened Bread. Nisan 15 was an "holy convocation," a Sabbath. The first and last day of Passover was, and still is, a Sabbath to the Jews. On this particular occasion, Nisan 15 is called "*an high day.*" From Jewish rabbis and teachers comes the definition of the term: It was given only to that Sabbath, the first day of the Passover Feast, or Passover Sabbath, which occurred on the regular weekly Sabbath day, the seventh day of the week.

"The Jewish people have 11 Sabbaths during their calendar year today which are designated by special names either because of special reading of the Torah and Prophets, or on account of some related historic incident. One of these is called *Shabbos Hachodesh* (the Sabbath of the Month). *This Sabbath introduces Nisan* and occurs on the 15th day, (the 14th being the day of the Passover sacrifice). The special Torah reading in the synagogue is taken from Exodus 12:1-20 at that time."[40]

"'The Jews therefore, because it was the preparation; that is, the day before the sabbath' (Mark 15:42). This note of time certainly blends both the synoptists and John in the assurance

---

[39]James Hastings, *Dictionary of the Bible.*
[40]A.M. Heller, *The Vocabulary of Jewish Life.*

that the crucifixion took place on a *Friday*. There was a twofold sanctity about that particular sabbath, seeing that the sabbatical rest of the day following the Paschal meal coincided with the ordinary weekly sabbath; (for 'great,' or 'high,' was the day of that sabbath) (cf. Exodus 12:16; Leviticus 23:7)."[41]

"John 19:31. Here we have reference to the *Preparation* and also to the *Sabbath* which, in this case, was a 'high day.' This shows that the Passover (the legal observance) was eaten on Friday evening after sunset on the 15th of Nisan at the beginning of the Jewish Sabbath. Whenever the Passover fell upon the Sabbath, that Sabbath was a 'high day'."[42]

"There was a twofold sanctity about the coming day, for it was not only the day at the beginning of which in the evening the passover lamb was eaten–it was at the same time the weekly Sabbath, and therefore a day of peculiar sanctity, *a high day.* Hence the anxiety of the Jews to hasten the death of the crucified."[43]

[41]Spence and Exell, *The Pulpit Commentary*, volume 17.
[42]*The International Standard Bible Encyclopaedia.*
[43]Rev. W. Frank Scott, *The Preacher's Homiletic Commentary* [John].

# New Evidence–The Dead Sea Scrolls

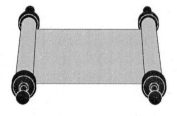

The recent discovery of the Dead Sea Scrolls[44] is one more proof of the truth of God's Holy Word. From the following quotations about this ancient document given by commentators, we gather some information about the *time* of the crucifixion of Messiah:

"At Qumran, the community was observing a different calendar from that in use in Jerusalem. Thus, in their eyes, all the Temple ritual there was being observed on the wrong days of the year and its efficacy thus hopelessly impaired."[45]

"As most probably for the Qumran Sect, this Last Supper, according to a strong tradition, was a Passover ceremony. Jesus used the older, *priestly* calendar. The Qumran Covenanters would have been celebrating their Passover on the Tuesday night … with the support of a tradition contained in the third century '*Didascalia*,' that it was then Jesus held His Last Supper with His disciples, three days before His crucifixion and the orthodox observance of the Passover."[46]

---

[44]Theodor H. Gaster, *Translation of the Dead Sea Scriptures.*
[45]J.M. Allegro, *The Dead Sea Scrolls,* p. 113.
[46]*Ibid,* p. 146.

Jesus followed the *priestly* calendar, not the calendar of the Qumran Sect (except for this last Passover which, of necessity, had to be observed one day in advance). If the Qumran Sect celebrated their Passover Feast on Tuesday night and the orthodox calendar showed this holiday to be *three days later,* then *Friday* would be the **day** of the *sacrifice* and *Friday* **evening** the Passover *Feast* officially began!

# SECTION 3
# THE SABBATHS

## SATURDAY, NISAN 15 (Friday evening)

### SOLDIERS BREAK LEGS OF THE TWO THIEVES/PIERCE SIDE OF JESUS

### *John 19:32-37*

32. *Then came the soldiers, and brake the legs of the first, and of the other which was crucified with him.*
33. *But when they came to Jesus, and saw that he was dead already, they brake not his legs:*
34. *But one of the soldiers with a spear pierced his side, and forthwith came there out blood and water.*
35. *And he that saw it bare record, and his record is true: and he knoweth that he saith true, that ye might believe.*
36. *For these things were done, **that the scripture should be fulfilled**, A bone of him shall not be broken.*
37. *And again **another scripture saith**, They shall look on him whom they pierced.*

It was the custom at that time that the bones of the legs of those crucified were to be broken. This prevented them from standing up on the small ledge beneath them to "catch their breath," and thus their death was brought about by suffocation. This custom, however, was not carried out with Jesus since He had expired before the soldiers came to Him. This also was in fulfillment of God's command concerning the lamb: *"... neither shall ye break a bone thereof"* (Exodus 12:46).

The command of God not to break the bones of the lamb is observed today especially by the Samaritans in Israel. They roast the lamb on a cross-shaped pole so as to observe these directions, and eat the meat as they hold it with their fingers. They fear that the use of knife and fork would "endanger the bones" and so break God's commandment!

### JOSEPH ASKS PILATE FOR BODY OF JESUS

#### Matthew 27:57-58

57. *When the even was come, there came a rich man of Arimathaea, named Joseph, who also himself was Jesus' disciple:*
58. *He went to Pilate, and begged the body of Jesus. Then Pilate commanded the body to be delivered.*

#### Mark 15:42-43

42. *And now when the **even** was come, because it was **the preparation**, that is, the day before the sabbath,*
43. *Joseph of Arimathaea, an honourable counsellor, which also waited for the kingdom of God, came, and went in boldly unto Pilate, and craved the body of Jesus.*

## "Even"

The Greek for even (evening) is *opsias*. The Jews of the New Testament period understood by *opsias* the time commencing with the setting of the sun (Mark 1:32) and the ushering in of the new Jewish day, from six o'clock on. It meant the same to them as the Hebrew word used in Leviticus 23:32: *"... in the ninth day of the month at even, from even unto even, shall ye celebrate your sabbath."* The evening watch included the period from six to nine o'clock. Thayer gives the translation of *opsias* as *evening*, then adds, i.e., either from our three to six o'clock p.m., or from our six o'clock p.m. to the beginning of night. The form of the verb employed with *opsias de genomenes*, properly translated, "And evening being come." It is interesting to note in this connection *The Twentieth Century New Testament* translates Mark's phrase, "When it was *already* evening." In

71

other words, the new day, Nisan 15, *had already started* before Joseph went to Pilate to ask for the body. *And the body was still hanging on the cross*!

## Luke 23:50-52

*50. And, behold, there was a man named Joseph, a counsellor; and he was a good man, and a just:*

*51. (The same had not consented to the counsel and deed of them;) he was of Arimathaea, a city of the Jews: who also himself waited for the kingdom of God.*

*52. This man went unto Pilate, and begged the body of Jesus.*

## John 19:38

*38. And after this Joseph of Arimathaea, being a disciple of Jesus, but secretly for fear of the Jews, besought Pilate that he might take away the body of Jesus: and Pilate gave him leave. He came therefore, and took the body of Jesus.*

At sunset, or the beginning of Nisan 15 (Saturday), Joseph of Arimathaea went to Pilate to ask for the body of Jesus. This was permissible on the Sabbath, for he was acting in an emergency.

### ANOINTING AND BURIAL

The Paschal lamb was to be consumed the night it was killed; nothing was to be left for the next day. *"And ye shall let nothing of it remain until the morning; and that which remaineth of it until the morning ye shall burn with fire"* (Exodus 12:10). *"...neither shall the sacrifice of the feast of the passover be left unto the morning"* (Exodus 34:25). *"His body shall not remain all night upon the tree, but thou shalt in any wise **bury him that day**; (for he that is hanged is accursed of God;)"* (Deuteronomy 21:23). The body of Messiah must be buried as quickly as possible after it was taken from the cross. Bodies had to be anointed, however, before interment. According to Jewish custom in Jerusalem, the dead were buried at night until recently.[47] The orthodox tradition is to bury the body without delay. Having the deceased "lie in state" for any length of time was (and is) completely foreign to Judaism. Therefore when the body of Messiah was taken down from the cross, it was buried *as soon as the body was anointed.* However, this was unlawful according to the *Mishneh* because, if Jesus were arrested at or just before the Feast, it would be necessary that He should be remanded in custody, in the "common prison" (Acts 5:18) for *nine days* until the Feast was over!

### *Matthew 27:59-60*

59. *And when Joseph had taken the body, he wrapped it in a clean linen cloth,*
60. *And laid it in his own new tomb, which he had hewn out in the rock: and he rolled a great stone to the door of the sepulchre, and departed.*

### *Mark 15:44-46*

44. *And Pilate marvelled if he were already dead: and calling unto him the centurion, he asked him whether he had been any while dead.*
45. *And when he knew it of the centurion, he gave the body to Joseph.*
46. *And he bought fine linen, and took him down, and wrapped him in the linen, and laid him in a sepulchre which was hewn out of a rock, and rolled a stone unto the door of the sepulchre.*

### *Luke 23:53-54*

53. *And he took it down, and wrapped it in linen, and laid it in a sepulchre that was hewn in stone, wherein never man before was laid.*

---

[47]Jacob DeHaas, *The Encyclopedia of Jewish Knowledge.*

*54. And **that day was the preparation,** and **the sabbath drew on.***

"The sabbath drew on" = "The sabbath began to grow toward daylight" (Greek text) and thus the preparations for burial and the entombment of the body of Jesus had taken place when Nisan 14 had ended–at night–which was the beginning of their Sabbath or the 15th of Nisan. It was a hurried affair on account of the near approach of the Sabbath daytime. Careful examination of the Greek text indicates that they were largely concerned that the bodies should not remain on the cross during the *daytime* of the following day. The explanatory clause of John 19:31 reads, literally: "...for the *day* of that sabbath was a great (one)," indicating the *daytime* of the day, rather than the entire 24 hours. (The Hebrew term *day* can mean the warm hours of the day and also can be the period from sunset to sunset, as well as from sunset to *sunrise*!) It was the duty of the Roman soldiers to remove the bodies from the cross or see that it was done (and this they did *only* at night as previously mentioned). They would do this no matter what time of night it was, as long as these bodies were not hanging on the crosses during the *daytime* of the following Sabbath day.

### John 19:39-40

39. *And there came also Nicodemus, which at the first came to Jesus by night, and brought a mixture of myrrh and aloes, about an hundred pound weight.*
40. *Then took they the body of Jesus, and wound it in linen clothes with the spices, **as the manner of the Jews is to bury**.*

"It seems as if the 'clean linen cloth' in which the Body had been wrapped, was now torn into 'cloths,' or 'swathes,' into which the Body, limb by limb, was now 'bound' no doubt between layers of myrrh and aloes, the Head being wrapped in a napkin. Two disciples wrapped the body of Jesus with a hundred pounds of spices intermixed with the wrappings."[48]

---

[48]G. Campbell Morgan, *The Gospel According to John.*

John is careful to say they buried Him "as the custom of the Jews is to bury." That is to say not after the Egyptian manner, or the manner of other nations, which meant embalming, and the mutilation of the body. The Jews never mutilated a dead body, but wrapped it in spices in the cloths, and last of all a final winding sheet. The wrapping of those dead bodies was a work of singular complexity.

"Burial followed generally as soon as possible after death (Acts 5:5-6, 10; 8:1-2), no doubt partly on sanitary grounds. The preparations for the burial of our Lord, mentioned in the Gospels: the ointment against His burial (Matthew 26:12), the spices and ointments (Luke 23:56), the mixture of myrrh and aloes, find their literal confirmation in what the Rabbis tell us of the customs of the period (*Ber.* 53a)."[49]

Jews were forbidden to embalm their dead to prevent decay as the unbelievers did. The rapid decomposition of the body in that climate demanded *immediate* burial. The body of Messiah, though dead (He gave up the ghost), hung on the cross in the sun from 3 p.m. until after sundown before it was prepared for burial and placed in the tomb. His body could not be held over for one day before entombment or remain a full 72 hours in the grave, for in that time it would have become *entirely* corrupted. This would have been contrary to Messiah's prophecy: *"Thou wilt not suffer* [permit] *thine Holy One to see corruption,"* which is spoken of His flesh! (See Psalm 16:10; Acts 2:31.)

"Dead bodies, after a revolution of the humours (originally, any of the four bodily fluids: blood, phlegm, choler, or yellow bile, and melancholy, or black bile) which is completed in 72 hours, naturally tend to putrefaction" (Dr. Hammond).

Messiah's body bore our sins (1 Peter 2:24) and in the sinner's stead, "tasting of death" (both physical and spiritual)

---

[49]Alfred Edersheim, *In the Days of Messiah.*

would have undergone the same experience as every dead body by the fourth day. But He arose before corruption could set in!

"The fourth day after death, the body is so altered that one cannot be sure it is such a person; ... Messiah rose *the third day* because He was not to *see* corruption.

"Psalm 16:10. The body shall lie but a little while in the grave; the body shall not continue dead so long as to begin to putrefy or become noisome; and therefore it must return to life **on** or **before** the third day after its death. He must die, for he must be *consecrated by his own blood*; but *he must not see corruption*, for his death was to be unto God of *a sweet smelling savour*. This was typified by the law concerning the sacrifice, *that no part of the flesh of the sacrifice which was to be eaten should be kept till the third day*, for fear it should see corruption and begin to putrefy, Leviticus 7:15-18."[50]

The apostles of Jesus had observed the Feast of the Passover at *sunset on Nisan 13* which was the beginning of Nisan 14, one day ahead of the legal observance, the 15th. But two loyal disciples, Joseph and Nicodemus, were not in the group on that occasion and had not as yet partaken of the Passover according to the commandment. Being defiled by the dead, they could not eat the Paschal Feast, but according to the law they thought they would eat it a month later. Numbers 9:5-12 explains conditions under which a person who is defiled by a dead body can participate in a Passover. The Lord makes a new law. He tells the people now that those defiled in this way can keep the Passover in the *second* month instead of the first month. (The Jews call this particular Passover *Pesach Sheni*, or "The Second Passover.") The Lord evidently had a definite purpose in making **this** particular law. He had in mind the death of His Son, the Lord Jesus, and He made provision for those who would handle that precious body at the time of the Passover! They did not realize at that time that they would not have to do this, for in a

---

[50]*Matthew Henry's Commentary.*

very peculiar way they had already partaken of the True Passover Lamb in the handling and burial of Him that very night!

### John 19:41-42

41. *Now in the place where he was crucified there was a garden; and in the garden a new sepulchre, wherein was never man yet laid.*
42. *There laid they Jesus therefore because of the Jews' preparation day; for the sepulchre was nigh at hand.*

THE WOMEN WATCH THE BURIAL/THEY REST THE SABBATH DAY

### Matthew 27:61

61. *And there was Mary Magdalene, and the other Mary, sitting over against the sepulchre.*

### Mark 15:47

47. *And Mary Magdalene and Mary the mother of Joses beheld where he was laid.*

### Luke 23:55-56

55. *And the women also, which came with him from Galilee, followed after, and beheld the sepulchre, and how his body was laid.*
56. *And they returned, and prepared spices and ointments; and rested the sabbath day according to the commandment.*

The women see how the body of Messiah is laid in the sepulchre after it has been taken down from the cross and anointed. Then they leave to prepare the spices to further honor the Dead. The women had watched at some distance and from where they stood could only have a dim view of what had transpired. It was not in accordance with Jewish manners for these women to have mingled more closely with the two *Sanhedrists* and their attendants. This explains how, on their return, they prepared spices and ointments for they hoped to give Messiah's body more full honors after the Sabbath was past.

Messiah taught that it was permissible to do emergency acts on the Sabbath; see Matthew 12:1-12. People must have died on various Sabbaths in those days and there was not one thing mentioned in the law against performing that which was necessary in such an event. The Jewish religious leaders wrote: "It is expressly allowed on Sabbaths and feast days to walk beyond the Sabbath limits, and to do all *needful offices for the dead*" (Jeremiah Ber. iii. I). The Mishnah (frequently used to designate the law which was transmitted orally) of the Jews allows the procuring, *even during the Sabbath,* of what is needed for the burial of the dead and also of *what is needed for the Passover!* The women then rest in the *daytime* of the Sabbath day.

**CHIEF PRIESTS REQUEST PILATE TO SEAL THE TOMB**

### *Matthew 27:62-66*

*62. Now the **next day**, that followed the **day of the preparation**, the chief priests and Pharisees came together unto Pilate,*

*63. Saying, Sir, we remember that that deceiver said, while he was yet alive, After three days I will rise again.*

*64. Command therefore that the sepulchre be made sure until the third day, lest his disciples come by night, and steal him away, and say unto the people, He is risen from the dead: so the last error shall be worse than the first.*

*65. Pilate said unto them, Ye have a watch: go your way, make it as sure as ye can.*

*66. So they went, and made the sepulchre sure, sealing the stone, and setting a watch.*

*"Jesus, when he had cried again with a loud voice, yielded up the ghost."* (Matthew 27:50)

*"He is not here: for he is risen, as he said. Come, see the place where the Lord lay."* (Matthew 28:6)

# SECTION 4
# THE DAY OF THE RESURRECTION

## SUNDAY, NISAN 16 (Sunday morning)

### THE WOMEN VISIT THE TOMB

"The burial was of necessity a very hurried one, which the holy women who witnessed it purposed to supplement by an anointing when the sabbath was past."[51]

### *Matthew 28:1-2*

1. *In the end of the sabbath, as it began to dawn toward the first day of the week, came Mary Magdalene and the other Mary to see the sepulchre.*
2. *And, behold, there was* [Greek = 'there had been'] *a great earthquake: for the angel of the Lord descended from heaven, and came and rolled back the stone from the door, and sat upon it.*

"In the end of the Sabbaths" (Greek text). That is, after the seventh-day and the Passover Sabbaths on Nisan 15 are over, and it is now *Nisan 16*, the women who had prepared their spices

---

[51]*The International Standard Bible Encyclopaedia.*

start off, while it is yet dark, on their journey to the tomb outside the city. They arrive at the tomb early Sunday morning. "The burial was of necessity a very hurried one, which the holy women who witnessed it purposed to supplement by an anointing when the sabbath was past."[52] The women visited the sepulchre as the custom was, partly to mourn and partly to pray (see John 11:13).

### Matthew 28:3-10

3. *His countenance was like lightning, and his raiment white as snow:*
4. *And for fear of him the keepers did shake, and became as dead men.*
5. *And the angel answered and said unto the women, Fear not ye: for I know that ye seek Jesus, which was crucified.*
6. *He is not here: for he is risen, as he said. Come, see the place where the Lord lay.*
7. *And go quickly, and tell his disciples that he is risen from the dead; and, behold, he goeth before you into Galilee; there shall ye see him: lo, I have told you.*
8. *And they departed quickly from the sepulchre with fear and great joy; and did run to bring his disciples word.*
9. *And as they went to tell his disciples, behold, Jesus met them, saying, All hail. And they came and held him by the feet, and worshipped him.*
10. *Then said Jesus unto them, Be not afraid: go tell my brethren that they go into Galilee, and there shall they see me.*

### Mark 16:1

1. *And when the sabbath was past, Mary Magdalene, and Mary the mother of James, and Salome, had bought sweet spices, that they might come and anoint him.*

---

[52]*Ibid.*

"See John 19:40. It is possible that they bought the spices on Friday just before the sabbath began (Luke 23:56), and prepared them after the close on Saturday evening."[53]

The following Scripture tells that it was very early on the first day of the week that the women go to the tomb. According to Jewish reckoning this would be the *third day* from His death (Friday, Saturday, Sunday). The relatives and friends of the deceased were in the habit of going to the grave up to the *third day* (when presumably corruption was supposed to begin), so as to make sure that those laid there were really dead (*Mass. Semach* viii p. 29d). Commenting on this, that Abraham viewed Mount Moriah *on the third day* (Genesis 22:4), the rabbis insist on the importance of "the third day" in various events connected with Israel, and specially speak of it in connection with the resurrection of the dead, referring in proof to Hosea 6:2 (*Ber. R.* 56. ed. *Warsh.* p. 102b). In another place, appealing to the same prophetic saying, they infer from Genesis 42:17, that God never leaves the just more than three days in anguish (*Ber. R.* 91). In mourning also, the third day formed a sort of period, because it was thought that the soul hovered around the body till *the third day*, when it finally departed from its earthly tabernacle (*Moed. K.* 28b; *Ber. R.* 100).

### Mark 16:2-8

2. *And very early in the morning the first day of the week, they came unto the sepulchre at the rising of the sun.*
3. *And they said among themselves, Who shall roll us away the stone from the door of the sepulchre?*
4. *And when they looked, they saw that the stone was rolled away: for it was very great.*
5. *And entering into the sepulchre, they saw a young man sitting on the right side, clothed in a long white garment; and they were affrighted.*

---

[53]*Irwin's Bible Commentary.*

6. And he saith unto them, Be not affrighted: Ye seek Jesus of Nazareth, which was crucified: he is risen; he is not here: behold the place where they laid him.

7. But go your way, tell his disciples and Peter that he goeth before you into Galilee: there shall ye see him, as he said unto you.

8. And they went out quickly, and fled from the sepulchre; for they trembled and were amazed: neither said they any thing to any man; for they were afraid.

### *Luke 24:1-11*

1. Now upon the first day of the week, very early in the morning, they came unto the sepulchre, bringing the spices which they had prepared, and certain others with them.

2. And they found the stone rolled away from the sepulchre.

3. And they entered in, and found not the body of the Lord Jesus.

4. And it came to pass, as they were much perplexed thereabout, behold, two men stood by them in shining garments:

5. And as they were afraid, and bowed down their faces to the earth, they said unto them, Why seek ye the living among the dead?

6. He is not here, but is risen: remember how he spake unto you when he was yet in Galilee,

7. Saying, The Son of man must be delivered into the hands of sinful men, and be crucified, and **the third day** rise again.

8. And they remembered his words,

9. And returned from the sepulchre, and told all these things unto the eleven, and to all the rest.

10. It was Mary Magdalene, and Joanna, and Mary the mother of James, and other women that were with them, which told these things unto the apostles.

11. And their words seemed to them as idle tales, and they believed them not.

### *John 20:1, 11-13*

1. *The first day of the week cometh Mary Magdalene early, when it was yet dark, unto the sepulchre, and seeth the stone taken away from the sepulchre.*

11. *But Mary stood without at the sepulchre weeping: and as she wept, she stooped down, and looked into the sepulchre,*

12. *And seeth two angels in white sitting, the one at the head, and the other at the feet, where the body of Jesus had lain.*

13. *And they say unto her, Woman, why weepest thou? She saith unto them, Because they have taken away my Lord, and I know not where they have laid him.*

**PETER COMES TO THE SEPULCHRE**

### *Luke 24:12*

12. *Then arose Peter, and ran unto the sepulchre; and stooping down, he beheld the linen clothes* [rather, "cloths," or bandages, in which the body of our Lord was wrapped with the spices] *laid by themselves, and departed, wondering in himself at that which was come to pass.*

### *John 20:2-7*

2. *Then she runneth, and cometh to Simon Peter, and to the other disciple, whom Jesus loved, and saith unto them, They have taken away the Lord out of the sepulchre, and we know not where they have laid him.*

3. *Peter therefore went forth, and that other disciple, and came to the sepulchre.*

4. *So they ran both together: and the other disciple did outrun Peter, and came first to the sepulchre.*

5. *And he stooping down, and looking in, saw the linen clothes lying; yet went he not in.*

6. *Then cometh Simon Peter following him, and went into the sepulchre, and seeth the linen clothes lie,*

7.  *And the napkin, that was about his head, not lying with the linen clothes, but wrapped together in a place by itself.*

It is claimed by Bible teachers and commentators that this "orderly arrangement of the grave clothes seems to have been the first thing to make the evangelist feel that Jesus must have risen from the dead."

## *John 20:8-10*

8.  *Then went in also that other disciple, which came first to the sepulchre, and he saw, and believed.*
9.  *For as yet they knew not the scripture, that he must rise again from the dead.*
10. *Then the disciples went away again unto their own home.*

**FIRST APPEARANCE OF JESUS AFTER RESURRECTION**

## *Mark 16:9-11*

9.  *Now when Jesus was risen early the first day of the week, he appeared first to Mary Magdalene, out of whom he had cast seven devils.*
10. *And she went and told them that had been with him, as they mourned and wept.*
11. *And they, when they had heard that he was alive, and had been seen of her, believed not.*

## *John 20:14-18*

14. *And when she had thus said, she turned herself back, and saw Jesus standing, and knew not that it was Jesus.*
15. *Jesus saith unto her, Woman, why weepest thou? whom seekest thou? She, supposing him to be the gardener, saith unto him, Sir, if thou have borne him hence, tell me where thou hast laid him, and I will take him away.*
16. *Jesus saith unto her, Mary. She turned herself, and saith unto him, Rabboni; which is to say, Master* [My Master-Teacher].

17. *Jesus saith unto her, Touch me not; for I am not yet ascended to my Father: but go to my brethren, and say unto them, I ascend unto my Father, and your Father; and to my God, and your God.*

18. *Mary Magdalene came and told the disciples that she had seen the Lord, and that he had spoken these things unto her.*

**JESUS APPEARS TO TWO DISCIPLES ON WAY TO EMMAUS**

### *Mark 16:12*

12. *After that he appeared in another form unto two of them, as they walked, and went into the country.*

### *Luke 24:13-21*

13. *And, behold, two of them went that same day to a village called Emmaus, which was from Jerusalem about threescore furlongs.*

14. *And they talked together of all these things which had happened.*

15. *And it came to pass, that, while they communed together and reasoned, Jesus himself drew near, and went with them.*

16. *But their eyes were holden that they should not know him.*

17. *And he said unto them, What manner of communications are these that ye have one to another, as ye walk, and are sad?*

18. *And the one of them, whose name was Cleopas, answering said unto him, Art thou only a stranger in Jerusalem, and hast not known the things which are come to pass there in these days?*

19. *And he said unto them, What things? And they said unto him, Concerning Jesus of Nazareth, which was a prophet mighty in deed and word before God and all the people:*

20. *And how the chief priests and our rulers delivered him to be condemned to death, and have crucified him.*

21. *But we trusted that it had been he which should have redeemed Israel: and beside all this, **to day is the third day** since these things were done.*

"This period seems to have been chosen by the Lord [Jehovah, in the type of Jonah] to associate the fact of resurrection with the *certainty* of death, so as to preclude all doubt that death had actually taken place, and shut out all suggestion that it might have been a trance, or a mere case of resuscitation. The fact that Lazarus had been dead 'four days already' was urged by Martha as a proof that Lazarus was dead, for 'by this time he stinketh' (John 11:17, 39). "We have to remember that corruption takes place very quickly in the East, so that 'the third day' was the proverbial evidence as to the certainty that death had taken place, leaving no hope."[54]

"There was no hope that His soul would return to His body, *after three days,* according to Jewish conception."[55]

'Three days since,' 'three days ago,' or three days from Sunday, Nisan 16 according to Jewish reckoning of time (a portion of a day as a whole) would be Friday, Nisan 14.

### *Luke 24:22-32*

22. *Yea, and certain women also of our company made us astonished, which were early at the sepulchre;*
23. *And when they found not his body, they came, saying, that they had also seen a vision of angels, which said that he was alive.*
24. *And certain of them which were with us went to the sepulchre, and found it even so as the women had said: but him they saw not.*
25. *Then he said unto them, O fools, and slow of heart to believe all that the prophets have spoken:*
26. *Ought not Christ to have suffered these things, and to enter into his glory?*
27. *And beginning at Moses and all the prophets, he expounded unto them in all the scriptures the things concerning himself.*

---

[54]*The Companion Bible.*
[55]Shepard, *The Messiah of the Gospels.*

28. And they drew nigh unto the village, whither they went: and he made as though he would have gone further.

29. But they constrained him, saying, Abide with us: for it is toward evening, and the day is far spent. And he went in to tarry with them.

30. And it came to pass, as he sat at meat with them, he took bread, and blessed it, and brake, and gave to them.

31. And their eyes were opened, and they knew him; and he vanished out of their sight.

32. And they said one to another, Did not our heart burn within us, while he talked with us by the way, and while he opened to us the scriptures?

**THE GREAT COMMISSION**

### *Matthew 28:18-20*

18. And Jesus came and spake unto them, saying, All power is given unto me in heaven and in earth.

19. Go ye therefore, and teach all nations, baptizing them in the name of the Father, and of the Son, and of the Holy Ghost:

20. Teaching them to observe all things whatsoever I have commanded you: and, lo, I am with you alway, even unto the end of the world. Amen.

### *Mark 16:15-18*

15. And he said unto them, Go ye into all the world, and preach the gospel to every creature.

16. He that believeth and is baptized shall be saved; but he that believeth not shall be damned.

17. And these signs shall follow them that believe; In my name shall they cast out devils; they shall speak with new tongues;

18. They shall take up serpents; and if they drink any deadly thing, it shall not hurt them; they shall lay hands on the sick, and they shall recover.

## Luke 24:46-49

46. *And said unto them, Thus it is written, and thus it behoved Christ to suffer, and to rise from the dead **the third day**:*

47. *And that repentance and remission of sins should be preached in his name among all nations, beginning at Jerusalem.*

48. *And ye are witnesses of these things.*

49. *And, behold, I send the promise of my Father upon you: but tarry ye in the city of Jerusalem, until ye be endued with power from on high.*

### THE ASCENSION

Messiah appeared to many for 40 days after rising from the dead. On the fortieth day He ascended into heaven and 10 days later poured out the Holy Spirit upon the 120 waiting disciples in the Upper Room.

## Mark 16:19

19. *So then after the Lord had spoken unto them, he was received up into heaven, and sat on the right hand of God.*

## Luke 24:50-51

50. *And he led them out as far as to Bethany, and he lifted up his hands, and blessed them.*

51. *And it came to pass, while he blessed them, he was parted from them, and carried up into heaven.*

"Christ died at the time the Passover lamb was slain on Friday afternoon, the 14th of Nisan, and thus became Our Passover (1 Corinthians 5:7). Jesus arose the third day and became 'the firstfruits of them that are asleep' (1 Corinthians 15:4, 20, 23). The resurrection was on the first day of the week. The sheaf, or firstfruits, was gathered *on Nisan 16*. Therefore Jesus must have died on Friday Nisan 14, when the Passover lamb was slain... All the early traditions, both Jewish and Christian, agree that Jesus was crucified on the day of Preparation."[56]

---

[56]*The International Standard Bible Encyclopaedia.*

# CHAPTER THREE
## From Passover to Pentecost

### *The First Double-Sabbath Day*

From the Scriptures we learn that the Passover was "the beginning of months." God instructed the Children of Israel that it was to be "the first month of the year" (Exodus 12:2). In order to keep this commandment, it was the practice of Israel to begin a new week each year with the Passover period. Nisan 15 was *always* the very *first* Sabbath for it was the day after the Passover sacrifice. It was called "an high day" for it was not only the Passover and Weekly Sabbath, the first day of the Feast of Unleavened Bread, but the beginning of *all* the weekly Sabbaths of the year.

### *Numbers 33:3*

3. *And they departed from Rameses in the **first month**, on the **fifteenth day** of the first month; on the **morrow after the passover** [sacrifice] the children of Israel went out with an high hand in the sight of all the Egyptians.*

### *Deuteronomy 5:14-15*

14. *But the **seventh day** is the **sabbath** of the LORD thy God: in it thou shalt not do any work, thou, nor thy son, nor thy daughter, nor thy manservant, nor thy maidservant, nor thine ox, nor thine ass, nor any of thy cattle, nor thy stranger that is within thy gates; that thy manservant and thy maidservant may rest as well as thou.*

15. *And remember that thou wast a servant in the land of Egypt, and that the LORD thy God brought thee out thence through a mighty hand and by a stretched out arm: **therefore** the LORD thy God commanded thee to keep the **sabbath day**.*

The foregoing two verses infer that Nisan 15, the *first day of Passover* or *Feast of Unleavened Bread,* a sabbath, was also the *weekly* Sabbath! On that first Passover which occurred in Egypt, the lamb was killed Nisan 14, the Children of Israel rested that night, and on the next day left the land of bondage. They traveled out of Egypt on Nisan 15, which later was to be a *double Sabbath day*!

## The Wave Sheaf

God told His people that after they settled in the land of Canaan, they were to keep another holiday on the "morrow after the sabbath," that is, the day after *Nisan 15*, the Passover Sabbath in which they were delivered from Egypt. This would be *Nisan 16.* In Leviticus 23:7 the Lord names the first day of Passover or Nisan 15, as a Sabbath, the seventh day of Passover, a Sabbath as well. Immediately following the commandment to keep the first and seventh days of *Passover* as a *Sabbath*, the Lord further instructs His people concerning His Feasts:

### Leviticus 23:9-11

9.  *And the LORD spake unto Moses, saying,*
10. *Speak unto the children of Israel, and say unto them, When ye be come into the land which I give unto you, and shall reap the harvest thereof, then ye shall bring a sheaf of the firstfruits of your harvest unto the priest:*
11. *And he shall wave the sheaf before the LORD, to be accepted for you: on the morrow after the sabbath the priest shall wave it.*

The Feast of First Fruits was to be observed "on the morrow after the sabbath." Notice very carefully that the Lord has been speaking of His *Feasts* and so *this sabbath* He refers to now is the **Passover** *Sabbath*! On this day after the Passover Sabbath (also the Weekly Sabbath), the Children of Israel were to bring a sheaf of firstfruits of their barley harvest and wave it before the Lord.

At the time of the commandment concerning the Feast of First Fruits, the Jewish people understood that they were to wave the sheaf and begin counting on *Nisan 15*, the day after the *Passover* (and Weekly) *Sabbath*. (The Jewish people follow this custom to the present time.)

The sentiment among the rabbis is universal that on Nisan 16 the wave sheaf was offered unto the Lord and this was the order of the services at the time of and during the second Temple. According to the rabbis the barley harvest began on Nisan 16 and the Feast of First Fruits is to be observed on that day[57]. "The Passover Sheaf was waved before the Lord on the *second Paschal day* (Nisan 16)."[58]

"On the second day of Unleavened Bread which is the *sixteenth day* of the month, they first partake of the fruits of the earth, for before that day, they do not touch them. And while they suppose it proper to honour God, from whom they obtain this plentiful provision, in the first place, they offer the first fruits of their barley, and that in the manner following: They take a handful of the ears, and dry them, then beat them small, and purge the barley from the bran; they then bring one tenth deal to the altar, to God; and, casting one handful of it upon the fire, they leave the rest for the use of the priest. And after this it is that they may publicly or privately reap their harvest. They also at the participation of the firstfruits of the earth, sacrifice a lamb, as a burnt offering to God."[59]

"'... *ye shall bring a sheaf of the firstfruits of your harvest unto the priest* (Leviticus 23:10).' The offering described in this passage was made on the 16th of the first month, and the day

---

[57]Jacob DeHaas, *The Encyclopedia of Jewish Knowledge.*
[58]Dr. Alfred Edersheim.
[59]Ben Edidin, *Jewish Holidays and Festivals,* page 166.

following the first Passover Sabbath, which was on the 15th, corresponding to the beginning of our April."[60]

On Nisan 14 at sunset (which now was "The Feast of Unleavened Bread," Nisan 15), the first service of the Passover week takes place. Then at the beginning of the harvest, the Jews bring an *omer* (Hebrew word for "a sheaf" or measure of grain) of barley on the *second day of Passover* (or Feast of Unleavened Bread, Nisan 16) as an offering of thanksgiving. It does not matter if the Passover happens to occur on the evening of Tuesday in our present secular calendar; it would still be Nisan 14 on the *Jewish* calendar and the beginning of Nisan 15 or Wednesday. Thursday then would be the second day (the 16th of Nisan, *Jewish* calendar), the morning after the Passover Sabbath, and on that day the sheaf of first fruits is waved before the Lord.

## *Day of Pentecost*

On that day also when the sheaf was waved before the Lord, they were to start to count the omer to the *fiftieth* day.

### *Leviticus 23:15-16*

15. *And ye shall count unto you from the morrow after the sabbath, from the day that ye brought the sheaf of the wave offering; seven sabbaths shall be complete:*

16. *Even unto the morrow after the seventh sabbath shall ye number fifty days; and ye shall offer a new meat offering unto the LORD.*

"The Pharisees who sought to interpret the Torah (Pentateuch) in accordance with the conditions of the day, interpreted the word *sabbath* as meaning not Saturday, but the day of rest, the *first day* of the festival. According to the Pharisees, therefore, it was necessary to offer the omer on the sixteenth day of Nisan,

---

[60]*Jamieson, Fausset and Brown Commentary.*

*Shavuos* (Hebrew word for *Weeks*. But the word for "seven" in Hebrew is *sheva*, from the same root we derive *weeks*. In other words the Feast of Pentecost was a period of *seven weeks* from the second day of Passover. [Greek word is *Pentecost*, which means fiftieth] coming on the sixth day of Sivan.)"[61]

"The festival of Shavuos has been observed on the sixth day of Sivan, the fiftieth day *after the second day of Passover*. This is further supported by the renderings of some of the oldest translations of the Bible, such as the *Septuagint* and the *Targum*, and by *Josephus*."[62]

"In the early days, when the Jews had no written calendar, the exact date of 'Shavuos' was figured by counting seven weeks from the *second day of 'Pesach'* (Passover), the holiday taking place on the fiftieth day." "Pentecost, the 50th day after Nisan 16, celebrating the completion of the corn harvest."[63]

"*Sefirah* ("counting," the counting of the omer). The *second day of Passover* was celebrated in ancient Palestine as the beginning of the barley harvest. In accordance with Leviticus 23:14, no part of the new crop might be eaten before that time when the first sheaf was harvested and offered as a sacrifice to God. The traditional Synagogue includes in the daily evening service an enumeration of the forty-nine days from that time until *Shavuos*, the festival of the wheat harvest."[64]

Not only from the foregoing information do we realize that the waving of the sheaf of first fruits could not have occurred on the day after the seventh-day Sabbath (except that that seventh-day Sabbath fell on the Passover Sabbath). But if we were to arrange the dates of the Jewish calendar to the present-day calendar we would arrive at the same conclusion. For example, let us suppose that Nisan 14 would fall on a Wednesday. If it

---

[61]Hayyim Schauss, *Jewish Festivals.*
[62]Julius H. Greenstone, *Jewish Feasts and Fasts.*
[63]James Hastings, *Dictionary of the Bible.*
[64]Abraham Heller, *The Vocabulary of Jewish Life.*

was after the *seventh-day Sabbath* that the Feast of First Fruits is to be observed, then it would be on the *fifth day* that the sheaf is brought before the Lord (Wednesday, 1; Thursday, 2; Friday, 3; Saturday, 4; Sunday, 5), when in actuality there was only an interval of *three* days (Jewish reckoning) between the killing of the Passover lamb and the waving of first fruits in the Temple! Therefore, let us remember that the Feast of First Fruits *always* has coincided with the day after *the Passover Sabbath* (which would now be the second day of the Passover Feast or The Feast of Unleavened Bread on Nisan 15), which *always* fell on the seventh-day Sabbath, and is so observed by Jews today.

## Fulfilled Old Testament Types

The types of the Passover season in the Old Testament were all fulfilled in Messiah Jesus. On Nisan 14 when the Jewish people were killing their lambs for the Passover Feast, Messiah the Lamb of God was crucified. Nisan 15 was the second day of the Feast of the Passover and the Feast of Unleavened Bread, also the seventh-day Sabbath (three-in-one). On the sixteenth of Nisan, three days after the Lamb of God was slain, the priest waved the *omer* before the Lord, "on the morrow after the sabbath." On that very day the Lord Jesus Messiah arose from the dead and became "the Firstfruits of them that slept" according to the prophecy. For 40 days He appeared or showed Himself to His disciples and on the fortieth day He ascended into heaven. This was the fortieth day of the counting of the Omer which began on the sixteenth of Nisan. Ten days after Messiah ascended into heaven, the counting of the Omer arrived at 50, the Day of Pentecost or Weeks. We read of the fulfillment of the type in the following words of Scripture:

## *Acts 2:1-4*

1. *And when the day of Pentecost was fully come* [the 50th day had arrived since Nisan 16; it was being fulfilled], *they were all with one accord in one place.*
2. *And suddenly there came a sound from heaven as of a rushing mighty wind, and it filled all the house where they were sitting.*
3. *And there appeared unto them cloven tongues like as of fire, and it sat upon each of them.*
4. *And they were all filled with the Holy Ghost, and began to speak with other tongues, as the Spirit gave them utterance.*

The "sign of Jonah," given by the Lord Jesus, was fulfilled exactly as He said. ***He died and rose again***! This is the foundation of our salvation! *"That if thou shalt confess with thy mouth the Lord Jesus, and shalt believe in thine heart **that God hath raised him from the dead, thou shalt be saved**"* (Romans 10:9).

# Calendars And Chart

In introducing the chart of Passion Week (and to Pentecost), "the relation of the Jewish night-days of the Paschal season to our days, which begin with midnight, will be apparent from the following scheme. This scheme accords with the theory that the Supper was instituted on the evening of the thirteenth and fourteenth Nisan."[65]

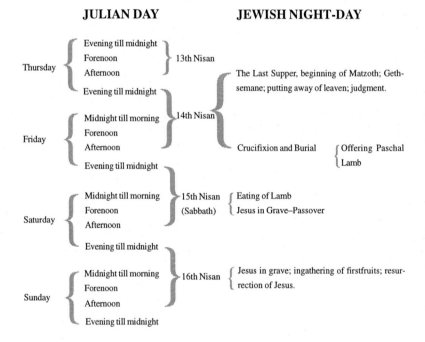

From Caspari's *Life of Christ.*

[65]Rev. W. Frank Scott, *The Preacher's Homiletic Commentary, John.*

# *Chart of Jewish Calendar*
## Passover to Pentecost

In the Jewish calendar, every month begins with the new moon and is composed of 29 or 30 days (alternately). The lunar month does not always begin on the same day as that of the solar year, and usually includes days from two different months according to the Western calendar.

**NISAN** (occurs in March or April)

| Sun. | Mon. | Tues. | Wed. | Thu. | Fri. | Sat. | |
|------|------|-------|------|------|------|------|---|
| | | | | Passover = **14** | | **15** | = Passover Sabbath |
| 16 - Counting of the Omer begins. | | | | | | | |
| **16** | **17** | **18** | **19** | **20** | **21** | **22** | = 1st Sabbath (of the omer) |
| **23** | **24** | **25** | **26** | **27** | **28** | **29** | = 2nd Sabbath |
| **30** | (15 Days of Counting the omer) | | | | | | |

**IYAR** (occurs in May)

| Sun. | Mon. | Tues. | Wed. | Thu. | Fri. | Sat. | |
|------|------|-------|------|------|------|------|---|
| | **1** | **2** | **3** | **4** | **5** | **6** | = 3rd Sabbath |
| **7** | **8** | **9** | **10** | **11** | **12** | **13** | = 4th Sabbath |
| **14** | **15** | **16** | **17** | **18** | **19** | **20** | = 5th Sabbath |
| **21** | **22** | **23** | **24** | **25** | **26** | **27** | = 6th Sabbath |
| **28** | **29** | (44 Days of Counting the omer) | | | | | |

**SIVAN** (occurs in June) (see Esther 8:9 = third month)

| Sun. | Mon. | Tues. | Wed. | Thu. | Fri. | Sat. | |
|------|------|-------|------|------|------|------|---|
| | | **1** | **2** | **3** | **4** | **5** | = *7th Sabbath* |
| **6** | *(Fiftieth Day of Counting)* | | | | **"Weeks" or "Pentecost"** | | |

# APPENDIX I

## Scroggie's Errors

I prepared the following article "Some Errors in *A Guide to the Gospels* by W. Graham Scroggie" not to defame this excellent teacher of God's Word, but to point out some difficulties in understanding the days and activities of Messiah's Passion Week which are *Jewish-oriented*. Page numbers listed are from the chapter in Mr. Scroggie's book entitled "The Day of the Crucifixion." (This study is to be used with Events of Passion Week chart, which follows this article.)

## *"The Day of Crucifixion"*

1.  **p. 570**. "Matthew 12:40…must mean three days, each preceded by a *night*…"

Messiah died on the DAY, not the night (the 9th hour or 3 p.m.) and the time begins to be counted from THAT moment He "gave up the ghost" and descended into the heart of the earth: that *day* the thief also descended to be with Messiah in Paradise as the Lord had promised! Too, if a complete *night* is intended, then, to be consistent, the *days* also must be complete. From 3 p.m. to 6 p.m. is not a complete day! Furthermore, if it was a complete 72 hours as Mr. Scroggie infers, then Messiah would have arisen on the FOURTH Day, not the THIRD!

2.  **p. 571, below diagram I:** "(Christ) said that His body would be there (in the tomb) for *three nights*."

Christ never said His *body* would be in the *tomb* for that period of time! He said He (Himself, i.e., His spirit-soul) would be *in the* heart of the earth [not the tomb] (Matthew 12:40). Immediately as He expired (the ninth hour or 3 p.m.), He *descended* into the *heart of the earth*, into *sheol*. His *body* was laid in a tomb *on the surface of the earth* several hours later! When Jesus told the thief *"Today"* he would be with Him in Paradise, that very day, the 14th Nisan, they were both in *sheol* (in the Paradise section) even as the Lord had promised.

3. In this section of his book ("The Day of the Crucifixion," **p. 572**) Mr. Scroggie lists many activities and asks how all these things could be accomplished in a three-hour period (assuming that this all had to be done before the Sabbath began). We can best understand this if we know that burial of the dead usually occurred at night and also that it was permissible even on the Sabbath! Too, when Joseph went to Pilate to ask for the body of Jesus (Mark 15:42-43) it is recorded: "When *even was come* because it was the preparation, that is the day before the *Sabbath...*" The Greek word is *"prosabbaton"* or "sabbath eve," "the before-sabbath." This definitely shows that it was the evening of the fourteenth (the preparation day in which the lambs were slain). The *evening* of the fourteenth would be the beginning of the fifteenth or the Passover and weekly Sabbaths. The Greek word "prosabbaton" or "sabbath eve," "the before-sabbath," agrees also with "when even was come" as the time when Joseph went to ask for the body of Jesus. It was *at night* that all these activities took place surrounding His burial, even though it was actually the beginning of the Sabbath. They would wash, anoint, wrap His body and bury it before the *daytime* of that (holy) "High Day"!

4. Mr. Scroggie confuses (as many do) "The Preparation Day" with the "preparation of the Passover." "The Preparation Day," "the day of the preparation," "the Jews' preparation," and "the preparation" are terms used to indicate work and arrangements for the seventh-day Sabbath. This particular *preparation day* ALWAYS fell on the *sixth* day of the week (Friday), *never* on any other day. Among orthodox Jews at present, this is still true. It is interesting to note also that the term "preparation" has been the regular name for *Friday* in the Greek language caused

by New Testament usage![66] If preparations were being made for any other holy day, *that holiday would be named,* such as we find in the following Scripture, for example: "And it was the preparation of *the passover*" (John 19:14).

5. **p. 573** "... markets were closed, spices and linen could not be bought; no labour could be hired or engaged in after the Sabbath had commenced."

For necessary work on religious holidays and Sabbaths, the *Old Testament* gives permission. Servile work (a person's secular employment, his regular occupation) was prohibited, but that service which was necessary such as anointing and burying the dead could be done on the Sabbath. The Pharisees sought to make the Sabbath-keeping more rigorous than God had commanded. Messiah rebuked them for this (Matthew 12:1-14; Mark 2:23-28; Luke 6:1-11). He told them to *do good* on the Sabbath; plucking corn was *work* but it was necessary to eating, etc. And besides, *would God have provided a SECOND PASSOVER* for those who had *handled* and *buried the dead* on the Passover Sabbath if *no one ever did* (see Numbers 9:2-14)? And, too, the *Mishnah* (in use in Messiah's day) expressly allowed the procuring, even on a Sabbath, what was needed for the Passover!

6. **p. 573**. Mr. Scroggie confuses (as many do) the *day* of the Passover sacrifice with the *night* of the Passover Feast. He quotes from Matthew 26:1-2 and Mark 14:1 using the words, "Feast of the Passover" when "*feast of the*" are words supplied by the translators. The Passover was *sacrificed* at 3 p.m. on 14th Nisan and *The Passover Feast* was observed in the evening of the 14th which began the new day, the 15th. He makes no distinction between the Passover **sacrifice** and the Passover **Feast**! Note: In these two portions of Scripture (Matthew 26:1-2; Mark 14:1) Messiah predicts that (in two days) He would be betrayed on the day of the Passover (sacrifice), the 14th Nisan,

---

[66]See W.E. Vine, *Expository Dictionary of New Testament Words*, under the word, "preparation."

and it was fulfilled on **that** very day. Messiah was betrayed by Judas in the beginning hours of that day, at night, in the Garden!

7.  **pp. 574-575**. In his chart Mr. Scroggie intimates (unintentionally, I am sure) that Messiah broke the Sabbath which, as a Jew "born under the law" (that is, He was in subjection to the law of God recorded in the Old Testament), "to fulfill all things," He would not do! He shows that Messiah traveled from Bethany to Jerusalem on the Sabbath day! Bethany (the actual city, not the geographical boundary) is located *"fifteen furlongs"* or 2 miles from Jerusalem (John 11:18)! Also on this same chart he indicates that the Tenth of Nisan was on a Saturday. The Tenth of Nisan was the time for selecting the lambs and setting them aside for examination involving much work which would not be consistent with his supposition that *no work* of any kind could be done on the Sabbath!

8.  **p. 575**. Mr. Scroggie states that the weekly Sabbath was never a "HIGH DAY."

John 19:31 states definitely that the weekly Sabbath was a "High Day" (Holy or Great Day)! It was understood by the Jews then (and today by orthodox Jews) that a "High Day" was always the first day of the Feast, as *a Sabbath*. John didn't have to say that the "High Day" was a Sabbath. It was already known as such. But he explained that this particular coming WEEKLY Sabbath was ALSO the First Day of the Feast, a "High Day"!

9.  **p. 575**. Mr. Scroggie assumes that the body of Messiah "laid in state" one whole day before it was "embalmed."

According to the custom of the Jews at that time the body of the dead did not "lie in state." Burial followed generally as soon as possible after death (Acts 5:5-6, 10; 8:1-2). The rapid decomposition of the body in that climate demanded *immediate* burial. They would not have placed the body of Messiah in the tomb unwashed from the blood and sweat, the bruises left to putrefy, the face, head, back, hands and feet with open sores. This is unthinkable! They would be careful to obey the commandment concerning those "hung on a tree" and bury Him *as soon as possible* after His death (see Deuteronomy 21:22-23)! Neither did the Jews *embalm* their dead; they washed, anointed and linen-wrapped the body "as the manner of the Jews was to bury." If they had allowed the body of Messiah to "lie in state" for one whole day in the tomb before anointing and wrapping it with linen as Scroggie infers, His body would have been corrupted, since it had hung in the hot sun for 6 hours until death and about 2 or 3 hours after death. This fails to agree with the prophecy that His flesh would see no corruption (see Psalm 16:10; Acts 2:31)!

Note: Concerning the *Linen Sheet and the Linen Wrappings* (or Bandages), see Matthew 27:59; Mark 15:46; Luke 23:53). The one piece of linen cloth ("*sindon*") was used in wrapping the body after taking it from the cross to carry to the tomb, where immediately afterwards, when preparing it for burial ("as the manner of the Jews was to bury"), Joseph and Nicodemus removed the "sindon", and bandaged the limbs and body in several linen cloths ("*othonia*") with spices (John 19:40), using a separate piece for the head (John 20:5-7; Luke 24:12).

10. Mr. Scroggie states that *Nisan 16* was the *Feast of Waving of First Fruits* and that Pentecost was Sivan 6 (**p.114**), yet on **p. 575** he states that Messiah rose after sunset on Nisan *seventeenth* which would then be Nisan *18*. If this is so, then Messiah did not fulfill the Feast of the Waving of Firstfruits which occurred on *Nisan 16*, the day after the Passover (and weekly) Sabbath. (The Passover Sabbath ALWAYS fell on the weekly Sabbath and is the Sabbath which begins all the Sabbaths of the Sacred New Year. It is closely associated with God's Rest. See Exodus 12:2, cf. Numbers 33:3; Deuteronomy 5:14-15.) On Nisan 16 the Jews were to begin counting to 50 days, reaching the fiftieth day on Sivan 6 when they were to observe the Feast of *Shavuot* (Seven Weeks) or Pentecost. The lunar month consisted of 29

and 30 days alternately so that, from 16 Nisan to 6 Sivan, there were 50 days, etc., etc.

11. **On page 584** we read these words of Mr. Scroggie: "The promise ["Today thou shalt be with me in Paradise"] distinguishes between the body and the spirit. The body of the robber was thrown into a hole, and the body of Jesus was laid in Joseph's tomb, but the spirits of both went, that day, to Paradise... He (Messiah) descended into Sheol, the Hebrew for the Greek Hades... Paradise (*paradeisos*) was one part of Hades, that part to which the blessed went; the other part for the wicked, being Gehenna (*geena*). That Paradise was in Heaven in Paul's time (2 Corinthians 12:2,4) implies that at the resurrection a change took place, and that Hades was emptied of Paradise."

Although Mr. Scroggie indicates here that Messiah (His spirit) descended into the "heart of the earth" on Nisan 14 the moment He died (3 p.m.), yet he begins to count the "three days and three nights in the heart of the earth" from the time of "embalming" the *body* and placing it in the *tomb* on the *surface* of the earth one day later!

# Events of Passion Week
# and on to Pentecost

(on following four pages)

(Chart designed by Ruth Specter Lascelle ©1972.)

(Chart revised and developed by Duane Bagaas, 1996.)

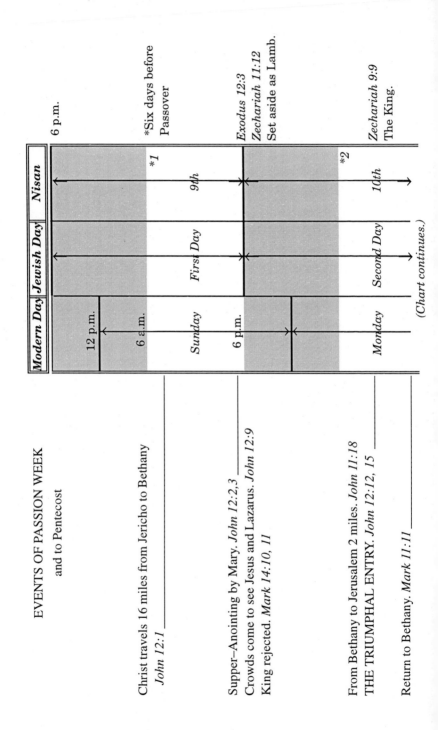

EVENTS OF PASSION WEEK
and to Pentecost

| Modern Day | Jewish Day | Nisan |
|---|---|---|

6 p.m.

*Six days before Passover

*1  9th

Exodus 12:3
Zechariah 11:12
Set aside as Lamb.

First Day

*2  10th

Zechariah 9:9
The King.

Second Day

12 p.m.

6 a.m.

Sunday

6 p.m.

Monday

(Chart continues.)

Christ travels 16 miles from Jericho to Bethany
John 12:1

Supper–Anointing by Mary. John 12:2,3
Crowds come to see Jesus and Lazarus. John 12:9
King rejected. Mark 14:10, 11

From Bethany to Jerusalem 2 miles. John 11:18
THE TRIUMPHAL ENTRY. John 12:12, 15

Return to Bethany. Mark 11:11

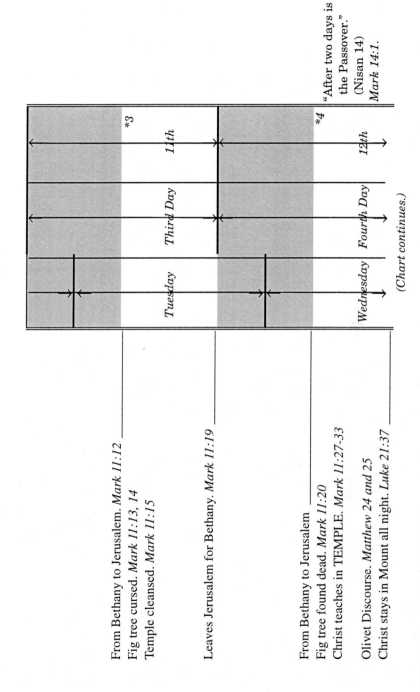

From Bethany to Jerusalem. *Mark 11:12*
Fig tree cursed. *Mark 11:13, 14*
Temple cleansed. *Mark 11:15*

Leaves Jerusalem for Bethany. *Mark 11:19*

From Bethany to Jerusalem
Fig tree found dead. *Mark 11:20*
Christ teaches in TEMPLE. *Mark 11:27-33*

Olivet Discourse. *Matthew 24 and 25*
Christ stays in Mount all night. *Luke 21:37*

*3

11th

Third Day

Tuesday

*4

12th

Fourth Day

Wednesday

*(Chart continues.)*

"After two days is
the Passover."
(Nisan 14)
*Mark 14:1.*

107

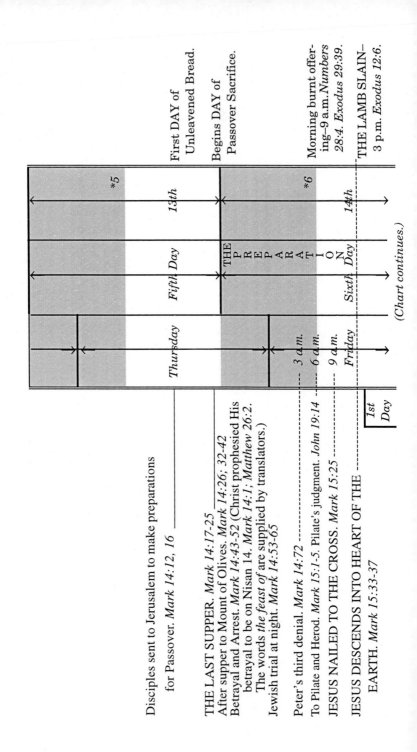

Disciples sent to Jerusalem to make preparations
for Passover. *Mark 14:12, 16*

THE LAST SUPPER. *Mark 14:17-25*
After supper to Mount of Olives. *Mark 14:26; 32-42*
Betrayal and Arrest. *Mark 14:43-52* (Christ prophesied His
betrayal to be on Nisan 14. *Mark 14:1; Matthew 26:2.*
The words *the feast of* are supplied by translators.)
Jewish trial at night. *Mark 14:53-65*

Peter's third denial. *Mark 14:72* ----------------- 3 a.m.
To Pilate and Herod. *Mark 15:1-5.* Pilate's judgment. *John 19:14* --- 6 a.m.
JESUS NAILED TO THE CROSS. *Mark 15:25* ---------- 9 a.m.
JESUS DESCENDS INTO HEART OF THE --------------
EARTH. *Mark 15:33-37*

First DAY of
Unleavened Bread.

Begins DAY of
Passover Sacrifice.

Morning burnt offer-
ing—9 a.m. *Numbers
28:4. Exodus 29:39.*

THE LAMB SLAIN—
3 p.m. *Exodus 12:6.*

*5

13th

*THE*
P
R
E
P
A
R
A
T
I
O
N

*Fifth Day*

*Sixth Day*

*6

14th

*Thursday*

*Friday*

*(Chart continues.)*

1st
Day

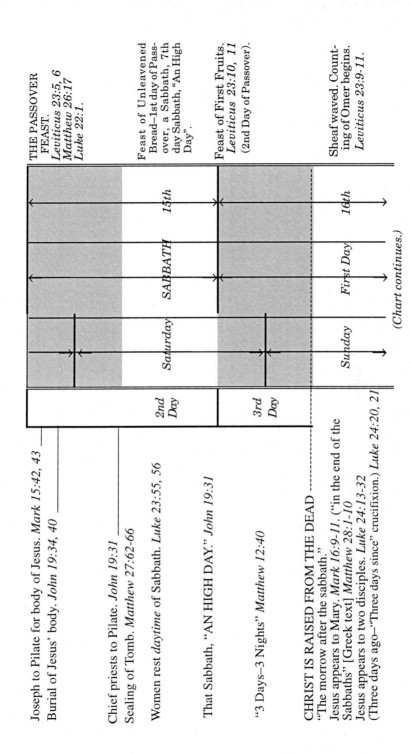

THE PASSOVER
FEAST.
*Leviticus 23:5, 6*
*Matthew 26:17*
*Luke 22:1.*

Feast of Unleavened
Bread—1st day of Pass-
over, a Sabbath, 7th
day Sabbath, "An High
Day".

Feast of First Fruits.
*Leviticus 23:10, 11*
(2nd Day of Passover).

Sheaf waved. Count-
ing of Omer begins.
*Leviticus 23:9-11.*

15th

16th

SABBATH

First Day

Saturday

Sunday

2nd
Day

3rd
Day

*(Chart continues.)*

Joseph to Pilate for body of Jesus. *Mark 15:42, 43*
Burial of Jesus' body. *John 19:34, 40*

Chief priests to Pilate. *John 19:31*
Sealing of Tomb. *Matthew 27:62-66*

Women rest *daytime* of Sabbath. *Luke 23:55, 56*

That Sabbath, "AN HIGH DAY." *John 19:31*

"3 Days—3 Nights" *Matthew 12:40*

CHRIST IS RAISED FROM THE DEAD
"The morrow after the sabbath."
Jesus appears to Mary. *Mark 16:9-11.* ("in the end of the
Sabbaths" [Greek text] *Matthew 28:1-10*
Jesus appears to two disciples. *Luke 24:13-32*
(Three days ago—"Three days since" crucifixion.) *Luke 24:20, 21*

109

*"And ye shall count unto you from the morrow after the sabbath, from the day that ye brought the sheaf of the wave offering; seven sabbaths shall be complete: Even unto the morrow after the SEVENTH SABBATH shall ye number fifty days; and ye shall offer a new meat [meal] offering unto the LORD."* Leviticus 23:15, 16.

| Days | | |
|---|---|---|
| 7 | Nisan 22 | 1st Sabbath of omer |
| 14 | Nisan 29 | 2nd Sabbath |
| 21 | Iyar 7 | 3rd Sabbath |
| 28 | Iyar 14 | 4th Sabbath |
| 35 | Iyar 21 | 5th Sabbath |
| **40** | Ascension -------- | |
| 42 | Iyar 28 | 6th Sabbath |
| 49 | Sivan 5 | 7th Sabbath |
| 50 | "Shavuot" (Hebrew) "Seven Weeks" –(Sivan 6) "Pentecost" (Greek) "Fiftieth" | |

THE MORROW AFTER THE SEVENTH SABBATH

# APPENDIX II

## Who Was Responsible for
## The Death of Christ?

(The following article is from my "Jewish Faith and the New Covenant," First Edition, pages 404-421.)

For the correct answer to the above question we do not inquire of any man but turn to the true Word of God which prophesies of the coming rejected Messiah of Israel and plainly tells us who would be His executioners:

> *"Why do the heathen rage, and the people imagine a vain thing? The kings of the earth set themselves, and the rulers take counsel together, against the LORD, and against his anointed, ..."* (Psalm 2:1-2).

Any student, understanding Bible language, will know immediately that whenever the word *heathen* is mentioned, it refers to unbelievers who were *Gentiles* at that time; that the word *people* refers to *Israel* (the Jews). The *kings of the earth* in the days of the execution of the Messiah, were *Gentiles*. The *rulers* were the Jewish religious leaders of the Jews. *His anointed*, of course, is the English translation of the Hebrew word "Messiah" and the Greek word "Christ."

From the foregoing Scripture then, we conclude that both Jews and Gentiles would be against God and His Messiah. In the book of Acts we discover the fulfillment of this prophecy:

> *"Who by the mouth of thy servant David hast said, Why did the heathen rage, and the people imagine vain things? The kings of the earth stood up, and the rulers were gathered together against the Lord, and against his Christ. For of a truth against thy holy child Jesus, whom thou hast anointed, both*

*Herod, and Pontius Pilate, with the Gentiles, and
the people of Israel, were gathered together"* (Acts
4:25-28).

## The Gentiles

Since the Gentiles are the first group mentioned in the foregoing Scripture, we will consider them first.

*"But we speak the wisdom of God in a mystery,
even the hidden wisdom, which God ordained before
the world unto our glory: Which none of the **princes
of this world** knew; for had they known it, **they
would not have crucified the Lord of glory**"*
(1 Corinthians 2:7-8).

The *princes* at the time of Messiah were *Gentiles*. Rome, a
Gentile city, controlled all the laws and governments of the then-
known world. She had power to sentence criminals, slaves,
foreigners, and traitors. Pilate, who was governor over the Jews,
was a *Gentile.*

Tarquin the Proud introduces *crucifixion* to the Roman world
from Phoenicia in the sixth century BCE (i.e., BC), therefore it
was a *Roman* method of execution. The Jewish method was
stoning (also burning, strangling, beheading for murder) according to the Law of Moses. There were 32 capital crimes, for which
there were four forms of execution. For the crimes of murder
and apostasy from Judaism to idolatry, the punishment was
beheading. Criminals convicted of the other 30 capital crimes
were put to death by stoning, burning or strangulation. Psalm
22 prophesies of the *Roman* manner of Messiah's death centuries
before Rome ever came into power, 250 years before this form
of execution was known and 1,000 years before it was fulfilled!
In this Psalm, through David, the Messiah predicts His own
crucifixion, even to the cry He would utter on the cross: *"My
God, my God, why hast thou forsaken me?"* (Psalm 22:1). Also
the word, *"done"* = *"He hath **done** this"* in verse 31, which

from the Greek New Testament is *"Tetelestai"* or *"It is **finished*** (done)!"* (John 19:30).

Let us notice another portion of this Psalm:

> *"Many bulls have compassed me: strong bulls of Bashan have beset me round. They gaped upon me with their mouths, as a ravening and roaring lion. I am poured out like water, and all my bones are out of joint: my heart is like wax; it is melted in the midst of my bowels. My strength is dried up like a potsherd; and my tongue cleaveth to my jaws; and thou hast brought me into the dust of death. For dogs have compassed me: the assembly of the wicked have inclosed me: they pierced my hands and my feet. I may tell all my bones: they look and stare upon me. They part my garments among them, and cast lots upon my vesture"* (Psalm 22:12-18).

In Psalm 22:16, Messiah (Christ) points out that the "dogs" and the "wicked" pierced His hands and His feet. (The Hebrew translation by Isaac Leeser is: "like a lion they threaten my hands and my feet." This *threatening* is translated as *pierced through* or *thrust through* as we see in the Hebrew text of Zechariah 9:9, *"They shall look up unto me whom they have **thrust through**, [pierced]."*

The Jews were God's "people," or the believers, and all who were not of "the commonwealth of Israel" were unbelievers, "heathen," "dogs," the "wicked." Dogs are incapable of receiving anything from heaven and the Gentiles were "strangers and foreigners" to God at the time of this prophecy. Messiah referred to the Gentiles as "dogs" on several occasions, but one in particular:

> *"For a certain woman, whose young daughter had an unclean spirit, heard of him, and came and fell at his feet: The woman was a Greek [Gentile], a*

*Syrophenician by nation; and she besought him that he would cast forth the devil out of her daughter. But Jesus said to her, Let the **children** first be filled: for it is not meet to take the children's **bread**, and cast it unto the **dogs**"* (Mark 7:25-27).

The "children" were the Jews, the "bread" was anything they received from God, and of course, the "dogs" were the Gentiles *at that time*. But thank God, now there is *no difference* between the Jew and the Gentile, *both* can come to the Father in heaven through Yeshua ha Meshiach (Jesus, the Messiah) for the middle wall of partition is broken down and the enmity done away in the Sacrifice on Calvary. However, we are considering the complicity in the death of the Messiah and we find in His own words that the Gentiles were to pierce His hands and His feet!

At the time of Messiah, the world was under the rule of Rome. This *Gentile* power determined the laws of the land and carried out the death sentence by crucifixion. Pilate was governor of Judea. He was a Gentile. He endeavored to escape from consenting to Messiah's execution but the Jews threatened to report him to Caesar. Afraid of losing his position as governor, he pronounced the death sentence of Jesus.

The most tragic part of the crucifixion was carried out by Pontius Pilate, a Gentile, to whom Jesus was delivered. The decision was utterly in his hand, yet after having declared He was innocent, he cowardly decreed His death (John 19:6-8, 19). He ordered his soldiers to crucify Jesus as the King of the Jews. This verdict was a *legal murder*, based upon falsehood. The crucifixion could only be carried out by the *Romans*. According to Josephus, Herod was tried for murder after the crucifixion of Jesus, because he "hath thereby transgressed our law, which hath forbidden to slay any man, even though he were a wicked man, unless he had been first condemned to suffer death by the *Sanhedrin*."

When the Messiah of Israel came to earth, He repeated the prophecy of His death to His disciples:

> *"And Jesus going up to Jerusalem took the twelve disciples apart in the way, and said unto them, Behold, we go up to Jerusalem; and the Son of man shall be betrayed unto the chief priests* [**Jews**] *...,and they* **shall condemn him to death,** *And shall deliver him to the* **Gentiles** *to mock, and to scourge, and to crucify him: ..."* (Matthew 20:17-19).

Notice the divine accuracy of this prediction: The *Jewish leaders* were to betray, condemn and deliver Messiah over to the Gentiles. The *Gentiles* were to mock, scourge, and crucify Him. We will see further how the *Gentile's* part was fulfilled even as the Lord had said.

> *"Then the* **soldiers of the governor** *took Jesus into the common hall, and gathered unto him* **the whole band of soldiers.** *And* **they** *stripped him, and put on him a scarlet robe. And when they had platted a crown of thorns, they put it upon his head, and a reed in his right hand: and they bowed the knee before him, and mocked him, saying, Hail, King of the Jews! And they spit upon him, and took the reed, and smote him on the head. And after that they had mocked him, they took the robe off from him, and put his own raiment on him, and led him away* **to crucify him"** (Matthew 27:27-31).

No Jew was permitted in the army of Rome. These soldiers consisted mostly of Italians, some Gauls (the present-day French), some Britons (the present-day American and British), and some Germans. In other words, this was a *Gentile*–not a Jewish–army. So it is that the *Gentiles* carried out in detail the prediction of the Messiah-Saviour concerning them in His own death. They did mock Him; they did scourge Him; and they actually did crucify Him!

## The Jews

Another group who were responsible for the crucifixion of Messiah Jesus were the "people" of Israel. Judas was a Jew. However, we must remember that the rest of Messiah's disciples, who loved Him and would have died for Him, were Jews as well! Messiah Yeshua chose twelve men to be with Him in His ministry. One who was trusted to carry the money bag, the treasurer of the group, one who dined with the Messiah, was prophesied to *betray* Him:

> *"Yea, mine own familiar friend, in whom I trusted, which did eat of my bread, hath lifted up his heel against me"* (Psalm 41:9).

> *"For it was not an enemy that reproached me; then I could have borne it:…But it was thou, a man mine equal, my guide, and mine acquaintance. We took sweet counsel together, and walked unto the house of God in company"* (Psalm 55:12-14).

This was fulfilled as written in the *Brit Hadasha* ("New Covenant"):

> *"And forthwith he* [Judas] *came to Jesus, and said, Hail, master; and kissed him. And Jesus said unto him,* **Friend***, wherefore art thou come? Then came they, and laid hands on Jesus, and took him"* (Matthew 26:49-50).

> *"But Jesus said unto him, Judas,* **betrayest** *thou the Son of man with a kiss?"* (Luke 22:48).

Betrayal speaks of mistrusted friendship. Jesus called Judas His *friend*. But Judas *betrayed* and *delivered* Jesus over to the Gentiles according to the prophecy!

# The False Arrest and Illegal Trial

The unfair trial of Messiah is not found recorded outside of the Gospels, for the Sanhedrin, knowing they acted illegally, were afraid to keep a record of it! According to the *Mishnah*, there were three Courts of Law in Jerusalem: the Greater Sanhedrin, the Lesser Sanhedrin composed of 23 members, and an Inferior Court or "Petty Court," "Court of the Three" composed of three members. The Greater Sanhedrin, the Court of One-and-Seventy Judges, was the Supreme Court of Appeal.

The Sadducees were the wealthy political aristocrats of the Jewish people. In the time of Jesus, the Temple and all local government was in the hands of the Saducean priests. The Sadducees dominated the Sanhedrin. They derived great wealth from the business side of the Temple services, involving as it did the sale of cattle and birds for the sacrifices, and the changing of money from Roman to Jewish currency. The Sadducees must have been particularly incensed when, on the Monday before His arrest, Jesus drove the money lenders and cattle dealers from the Temple.

The chief priests, elders and officers of the Temple arrested Jesus. Now it was a law at that time based upon the old law of Moses (Deuteronomy 17:6-7) that it was not legal for any member of the Sanhedrin to be an arresting officer. It was also illegal to arrest anyone after sundown no matter how bad a criminal he was, unless he were caught in the very act. He was absolutely safe under the law, until the following day. And then he could be arrested only by the witnesses. Furthermore, Jesus was really arrested by Judas and through his instigation, which under the law was not justified: *"Thou shalt not go up and down as a talebearer among thy people: neither shalt thou stand against the blood of thy neighbour: I am the LORD"* (Leviticus 19:16).

A witness had to be a person of good character; he was forbidden to take a bribe. A Gentile could not be a witness. An accomplice or accessory could not be a witness under any circumstances. Thus Judas could neither be a witness, nor arrest, because he was a companion, a traitor, a talebearer.

To take Jesus before Annas at night to be interrogated was absolutely illegal under the law, both because it was at night, and because no one person could legally interrogate either the accused or a witness. The Examining Board of the Sanhedrin had to consist of three to seven men; no one person could independently interrogate a witness or an accused person. It was also a law that a man could not incriminate himself. In other words, he could not suffer punishment or take a punishment upon his own confession; it had to be supported by the testimony of two or three witnesses (Deuteronomy 17:6; 19:15; Numbers 35:30).

The Sanhedrin could not have a trial before their Sabbath. Further, no trial could be held on a feast day, and this was the Passover week, in which every day was a feast day.

It was after midnight when Caiaphas questioned Jesus, who remained silent. As High Priest, Caiaphas could not interrogate any witness and could not express an opinion. Contrary to the law, he placed Jesus under oath and he sought to interrogate Him before any witness had been interrogated. Caiaphas, illegally putting Jesus under oath, said: *"...I adjure thee by the living God, that thou tell us whether thou be the Christ, the Son of God"* (Matthew 26:63). This question Jesus would answer because He could not deny Himself and He, therefore, replied: *"Thou sayest."* Then the High Priest expressed himself which he had no right to do, saying, *"You have heard him. He is guilty of blasphemy"* (Matthew 26:65; Mark 14:63-64; Luke 22:71).

The Sanhedrin violated the law on another term, when they spit in His face and struck Him. They committed physical violence (Mark 14:65). No judge could lay his hands on either a witness or the accused, or in any way violate his person.

Another illegal act was when Caiaphas at the end of the trial rent his garment which was, according to Leviticus 21:10 prohibited. The reason for this was that his priestly garment stood for the sacredness of his office.

It was personal feeling and jealousy which set the religious leaders against Jesus. For instance: when they saw that He was able to heal the incurable, they tried to charge Him with witchcraft (Matthew 9:24; 12:24; Mark 3:22; Luke 11:15). When He healed the man with the withered arm, they took occasion to impute to Him the profanation of the Sabbath (Matthew 12:9-13; Mark 3:1-6; Luke 6:6-11). When the Pharisees and Sadducees invited Him to dine with them, all their questions were directed to catch some words out of His mouth that they might accuse Him (Luke 11:37-57). When He reminded them that the Temple was God's house of prayer for all people (Isaiah 56:7) but that they had made it a den of thieves, they sought how they might destroy Him (Matthew 21:12-16; Mark 11:15-18; Luke 19:45-47). Their bitterest anger, however, which they could not restrain was when He raised Lazarus (John 11:43-45), for their own eyes gave them witness to the greatness of Jesus!

It was the Passover custom to release a prisoner from the jail in remembrance of the Freedom given to the Israelites on that first Passover. The Jews were given the choice as to which of two prisoners would be set free:

> *"But the chief priests [Jews] and elders [Jews] per-suaded the multitude [Jews] that they should ask Barabbas, and destroy Jesus. The governor answered and said unto them, Whether of the twain will ye that I release unto you? They said, Barabbas. Pilate saith unto them, What shall I do then with*

*Jesus which is called Christ? They all say unto him,* **Let him be crucified** [Here the Jews were condemning Jesus to death.] *And the governor said, Why, what evil hath he done? But they cried out the more, saying, Let him be crucified"* (Matthew 27:20-23).

Barabbas was a vile criminal according to the record: *"Who for a certain sedition made in the city, and for murder, was cast into prison"* (Luke 23:19). He deserved the sentence of death, but the Messiah who was innocent, who went about doing good, healing all those oppressed of the devil, took this murderer's place on the cross. Barabbas was set free because the Lamb of God offered Himself as a Substitute. Barabbas was loosed from the prison house and allowed to live because there was One who died in his stead. The Redeemer of mankind was the offering for sin, and though a man be vile, even as was Barabbas, a captive in the prison house of sin, he can come to the Saviour who will break the chains that bind him. God can and will loose the prisoner and bring him into the freedom of His wonderful Salvation! According to the divine prediction, the Jews *betray*ed, condemned Jesus, and delivered Him over to the Gentiles to moc*k*, to *scourge*, and to *crucify* Him.

There are other Scriptures which seem to imply only the Jews were to blame for Messiah's death (Acts 2:22-37; Acts 4:8-10; Acts 7:51-52; 1 Thessalonians 2:14-16). One particular portion of the Bible in the *T'nakh* (OT) actually names the Jews for the crucifixion of Messiah:

> *"And I will pour upon the* **house of David,** *and upon the* **inhabitants of Jerusalem**, *the spirit of grace and of supplications: and* **they** *shall look upon me* [look unto me] *whom* **they** *have pierced, and* **they** *shall mourn for him, as one mourneth for his only son, ... In that day there shall be a fountain opened to the* **house of David** *and to the* **inhabitants of**

*Jerusalem for sin and uncleanness. And one shall say unto him, What are these wounds in thine hands? Then he shall answer, Those with which I was wounded in the **house of my friends**"* (Zechariah 12:10; 13:1, 6).

According to the law of the land, an accomplice in a murder today is considered as guilty as the murderer. One hiring a crime done is as guilty as he who carried out the actual deed. The Gentiles were "hired" by the Jews to crucify Messiah Jesus. *Both* are guilty!

Though the Lord names both Jews and Gentiles as His executioners, yet it is the delight on the part of some who are uninformed, to point an accusing finger only at the Jewish people. The crucifixion of Messiah is used as a target for Jew-hatred and persecution. But we cannot judge the Jews for rejecting their Messiah any more than we can condemn the Gentiles for actually crucifying Him, for (as the prayer of the Messiah on the cross indicates) they did so in ignorance, and Messiah is ready to forgive *all* who come to Him and acknowledge their sin before Him!

It was the Pharisees (not all of them), the Sadducees who were against Him, and only a few individuals who could find room in the limited space of Pilate's court who shouted: "Crucify Him!" We note that of the 4.5 million Jews who existed in the day of Jesus, only 1.5 million lived in the Holy Land and in Jerusalem. The Jews that were scattered throughout Pontus, Galatia, Cappadocia, Asia, and Bithynia, and other places of their dispersion were not involved in the crucifixion of Jesus. God in His compassion was using as few as possible of His creatures to accomplish His purpose so that the doors of grace might remain open to all the rest of His children. Though Judas (Messiah's "trusted friend" turned into His bitterest enemy) was a Jew, yet the rest of the apostles were Jews as well. They were so devoted to the Master that they would have given their lives for Him!

Many claim that the persecution and the suffering visited upon the Jews today is because at the hour of crucifixion the people of Israel shouted: *"Let his blood be upon us and upon our children."* This was a wicked prayer (if it could be called a prayer) spoken by unbelieving men. *The blood of Jesus does not cry out for vengeance*! It was shed for cleansing from sin. The Lord took no notice of the aforementioned request for it was said in ignorance. Rather His great compassion was expressed when He cried: *"Father forgive them, for **they know not what they do!**"*

Israel, as a nation, would have been doomed and no Jew could ever be saved, *had they known He was the Messiah* and had rejected Him. When thousands of Jews were saved at Shavuot (Pentecost), the Lord's prayer of forgiveness on the cross was answered and is continuing to be answered whenever a Jewish person (or a Gentile) accepts Him as their Salvation!

## *The Devil*

However, there is another person responsible for the death of Jesus. We read of him in the very first promise of a coming Messiah. Speaking to the serpent, God said:

> *"And I will put enmity between thee and the woman, and between thy seed and **her seed** [Messiah]; it shall bruise thy head, and thou shalt bruise his heel"* (Genesis 3:15).

The serpent (Satan) was to bruise the heel of the Redeemer and, according to the prophecy this was done. Literally, in no other death (at that time) but crucifixion, would the heel of an individual actually be bruised! Messiah's heel was nailed (bruised) to the cross. It was fulfilled as His "heel" crushed the head of the Serpent (thereby defeating him by His death) and that "heel," in crushing the Serpent's head, was "bruised" according to the prophecy! It is Satan who seeks to thwart God's plan, to confuse the minds of the people. Satan it is who entered into the heart of Judas, planted hatred and aroused jealousy in the Sadducees and Pharisees. He stirred up all offenders and promoted Messiah's crucifixion.

## *Jesus*

But could not Jesus, as the Messiah, defend and deliver Himself from this death? Yes, He could have, but in doing this He would have opposed the whole plan of God for the salvation of the world. In refusing to go to the cross of shame, He would have failed in His task as Redeemer of mankind. Yeshua ha-Meshiah (Jesus, the Messiah) was responsible also for His own execution! The Scripture states:

> *"And being found in fashion as a man, he humbled himself, and became obedient unto death, even the death of the cross"* (Philippians 2:8).

He voluntarily, willingly gave His life as He said:

> *"I am the good shepherd: the good shepherd giveth his life for the sheep. Therefore doth the Father love me, because I lay down my life, that I may take it again. No man taketh it away from me, but **I lay it down of myself.** I have power to lay it down, and I have power to take it again. This commandment have I received of my Father"* (John 10:11, 17-18).

Jesus was not forced to die. He consented to it, for His Father had so commanded. When Peter took a sword and used it to defend his Master, Jesus rebuked him: *"...Put up thy sword into the sheath: **the cup which my father hath given me, shall I not drink it?**"* (John 18:11). It was prophesied in the *T'nakh* (OT) that the Messiah would give Himself over to suffering and death: *"I gave my back to the smiters, and my cheeks to them that plucked off the hair: I hid not my face from shame and spitting"* (Isaiah 50:6). Yes, Jesus gave His head to wear the thorns for you; He gave His cheeks to be smitten for you *"He giveth his* *cheek to him that smiteth him: …"* (Lamentations 3:30). He gave His eyes to weep over your sins; He gave His tongue to pray for you; for you He gave His back to be ploughed *"The plowers plowed upon my back: they made long their furrows"* (Psalm 129:3), for you He gave His side to the spear; He gave His hands to the cruel nails and He gave His soul, an offering for you. Yes, He clothed Himself in a human body that He might have it to offer (Hebrews 10:5, 9-10). He became possessed of a human heart that it might be broken. He partook of blood which flowed in His veins in order that He might give it for the life of the world!

## *God*

But there is Someone else without whom there could have been no crucifixion for Messiah. It was by the determinate counsel and foreknowledge of *God*, that the Messiah was "cut off." Jews and Gentiles "were gathered together" against Jesus *"… to do whatsoever thy* [God's] *hand and thy* [God's] *counsel determined before to be done"* (Acts 4:28). God Himself was responsible for the death of Messiah! In the very beginning it was *God* who slew an animal in the Garden of Eden, shedding its blood, in order to make coats of the skin to cover Adam and Eve. This prefigures the Great Sacrifice which the great Creator was to give for the redemption of the world. Before the creation of the world it was in the mind of the Father that the Messiah would come to be a Substitute, to die in order that those believing in Him could live. The Lamb was slain before the foundation of the earth by the determinate counsel of God!

> *"… the LORD hath laid on **him** [Messiah] the iniquity of us all. Yet it pleased* [was the will of] *the LORD to bruise him [Messiah]; **He** hath put **him** to grief: when thou [the Lord God] shall make his soul an offering for sin …"* (Isaiah 53:6, 10).

Who bruised the Messiah, put Him to grief, and made His soul an offering for sin? *The Lord God!* The Messiah Himself foretold that *God* would put Him to death: *"...and **thou** [referring to the Lord] hast brought me into the dust of death"* (Psalm 22:15). God could have prevented that awful scene at Golgotha! He could have sent a legion of angels in defense of Jesus! He could have, but (as it is written): *"He spared not his own Son, but"* Why? Because He *"delivered him up for us all ..."* (Romans 8:32).

At the trial of Jesus, Pilate declared to Him that he had the power to release or to crucify Him. *"Jesus answered, Thou couldest have no power at all against me, except it were given thee **from above** ..."* (John 19:11; Hebrews 10:5, 9-10). Not only did God give power to Pilate, but to the Jews and the Gentiles, using them as human instruments to accomplish His purpose. God gave power to Satan that he might push forward this execution. And yes, God gave power to Jesus to lay down His life!

> *"God so loved the world, that he **gave** his only begotten Son* [as a sacrifice], *that **whosoever** [Jew or Gentile] believeth in him should not perish, but have everlasting life"* (John 3:16)!

The crucifixion is not a record of an historical misunderstanding; not a tragic event which ended in defeat. The cross is a fulfillment of a divine decree made before the foundation of the world! *The death of the coming Messiah is prophesied, and we see the manner of that death portrayed in type and symbol throughout the T'nakh, the Old Testament!* The furniture of the Tabernacle of Moses, which was designed by God, was directed by God to be placed in such a way that it formed a cross! When the Israelites were commanded to take up the Tabernacle to travel to another place which the Lord would show to them, they were to march with the furniture in cross formation. When the people of Israel were to observe that first Passover in Egypt, they were to kill an innocent lamb, then take the blood and strike it, not just in any way they pleased, but on the two sideposts and the upper doorpost of their houses. Taking the blood from the basin on the threshold to the upper door post and on the two side posts shows that it was struck in the fashion of a cross!

## Everyone

"The crucifixion is an event in which the whole world took part. Jewish disciples and well-wishers forsook Him and fled; Gentiles spat upon Him and mocked Him. Jews delivered Him to Pontius Pilate; Gentiles nailed Him to the cross. Jews cried, 'Crucify!' Gentiles gambled on His vesture. Messian Jews wept at the foot of the cross; Gentiles crushed the crown of thorns on His brow. Christian Jews brought costly spices; Gentiles offered Him vinegar and gall. Christian Jews were His pallbearers; Gentiles pierced His side. Thus Jews *and* Gentiles crucified our Lord" (A.J. Kligerman).

## The Guilty One

Who plaited the crown of thorns for His brow?
Some Roman soldier, nameless now.
Who hewed the Cross from the grim pine-tree?
Some Jew, a carpenter as was He.
Who forged the nails He was fastened with?
He knew no better, poor nameless smith.
Nameless all, for the sin and shame
Were done by the one that bears my name.
*–Father Hugh Blunt, L.L.D.*

A man dreamed of seeing Jesus being led out to be scourged. He saw the Saviour's back laid bare and a rough soldier inflicting bloody stripes upon His flesh. Again and again the lash rose and fell. At length the sleeper could bear no more. In his dream he rushed forward, caught the upraised hand, spun the soldier around, and–looked into his own face!

No one is exempt from responsibility in the death of Messiah! Though chapter 53 of Isaiah, the Jewish prophet, is written concerning the Messiah of Israel and Israel's rejection of Him, yet it deals also with *all* sinners in relation to the Saviour:

> *"Surely he hath borne **our** griefs, and carried **our** sorrows: ... But he was wounded for **our** transgressions, he was bruised for **our** iniquities: the chastisement of **our** peace was upon him; ...for the transgression of **my people** was he stricken. ...for he shall bear **their** iniquities ...and he bare the sin of **many**, ..."* (Isaiah 53:4, 5, 8, 11, 12).

**The entire world is guilty** before God of the crucifixion of Messiah. His suffering and death was necessary for our salvation. According to the Divine Plan the *Innocent One* must die in order that we might live. He must be made sin in order that we might be made righteous. He must suffer the wrath and judgment of the Almighty God in order that we might be reconciled to our Maker. This One who is the Substitute, the Sacrifice and Ransom is Jesus, the Messiah and we (Jew and Gentile) who believe upon Him by accepting Him into our heart are pardoned for our sin and receive His life and righteousness!

# APPENDIX III

## Easter And Anti-Semitism

from *The International Christian Embassy,*
Jerusalem, Israel

Easter is the season when the Church proclaims that Jesus rose from the dead. For Christians it is a time of rejoicing for Messiah's victory over sin and death. For Jews, Easter has meant something completely different. For them, in many parts of Christendom, Easter became a time of fear, persecution and often death. In Eastern Europe and Russia, pogroms at Easter were common. Mobs, inflamed by Good Friday sermons, attacked Jews to avenge the death of Jesus.

Since the beginning of Church history, *some* Christians have held Jews responsible for the death of Jesus: not only the Jews of the First Century, but every generation since. Nothing has harmed the Jewish people more than the charge of *deicide*, as Christians historically have taken it upon themselves to punish the Jews.

This tragedy has partially resulted from an ignorance of Scripture. Jewish religious leaders were involved in Christ's death, but the New Testament does not hold the Jewish people responsible for the crucifixion. Jesus explicitly forgave both Gentiles and Jews who took part in crucifying Him (Luke 23:24), but the Church seems to have overlooked this prayer. Instead, the cry of an ignorant mob has been emphasized: "His blood be on us, and on our children" (Matthew 27:25). In Peter's sermon in the book of Acts, he tells a Jewish audience that he knows they acted in ignorance, but this is how God fulfilled what was foretold in the prophets (Acts 3:17).

While many Christians blame all Jews for the death of Jesus, the role of the Romans has scarcely been remembered. The Nicene Creed includes the phrase, "Suffered under Pontius Pilate," thus assigning responsibility to the Romans. Many Christians look on Pilate sympathetically, and the Coptic Church of Egypt even makes him a saint! History records him as a man of violence and brutality. Nonetheless, no one seriously holds the Italians responsible for the crucifixion.

Scripture teaches that it was *God* who smote Jesus to bring about our redemption: "Smitten of God, and afflicted. But He was pierced through for our transgressions … but the Lord was pleased to crush Him, putting Him to grief" (Isaiah 53:4-5, 10). Ultimate responsibility for Christ's death lies with each member of the human race who, being locked into sin, needs a redeemer (Romans 2:23-24).

At the time of Jesus, the Roman world was rife with hatred of Judaism [the Jews' religion]. Approximately 10% of the Roman Empire was Jewish. Such a large community attracted hostility for their refusal to worship Roman gods, intermarry or kill their physically handicapped children–a common Roman practice. Christian hostility toward Judaism and the charge of deicide began as large numbers of non-Jews converted to Christianity. These converts brought with them the anti-semitism of their pagan background, creating within the early church a distorted attitude toward the Jewish people.

By the end of that century, the split between church and synagogue had become unbridgeable, and the two faiths began competing for converts. During this period a number of myths were formulated to discredit the Jews, most notably the myth of their responsibility for the death of God. Closely related was the assumption that Jerusalem was destroyed and the Jews scattered because they rejected Jesus. Like much traditional Church teaching on the Jews, this has little support in the New Testament, which makes no direct connection between Jesus' death and the destruction of Jerusalem in 70 A.D. Jesus foretold the coming desolation of the city, but did not draw a connection between His death and the approaching national calamity. *There also is no evidence that the Jews were dispersed because they rejected Jesus.* **Nearly 80% of the people were** *already* **scattered throughout the world by this time!**

Despite the suffering caused by Christians blaming the Jewish people for the death of Christ, the myth of corporate Jewish guilt continues. It is transmitted by churches, theological colleges, missionaries, through Passion Plays and the media. Father Jean Paul Lichtenberg, in his short "History of the Relations Between Jews and Christians," suggests that the Church threw upon the Jews the responsibility for Christ's death because *"it was too heavy for the Christian conscience to carry ..."* In making the Jewish people the scapegoat of Christianity, the Christians probably unburdened their conscience. It was not they who were guilty, but those Jews, 'castigated' and 'cursed' by God, who might thus be attacked. The Crusaders who massacred thousands of Jews must have reasoned in this manner ..."

The Holy Spirit is saying to the Church in this generation: "Repent of your anti-semitism and make restitution to the Jewish people." Let us heed this call and act upon it.

*–The Jerusalem Post*

# APPENDIX IV

## Jesus Before The Bar

by

Dr. A.U. Michelson,

former Jewish Judge in Germany,

Founder-Pastor of the First Hebrew-Christian Synagogue,

Boyle Heights, Los Angeles, California,

Editor of *The Jewish Hope* Magazine.

(Date of this article, *circa* 1936)

> Dr. Michelson gave credit to the following for excerpts he used in his composition: *J.E. Spooner* in *The Unlawful Trial of Jesus,* E. Fischbein in *The Trial of Jesus,* F.C. Gilbert in *Practical Lessons,* Edersheim in *The Trial of the Christ,* D. Baron in *The Doctor of the Law* and *We Have Found the Messiah,* I. Lichtenstein in *An Appeal for the Jewish People,* Andrew Murray in *The Power of the Blood* and *The Student's Commentary on the Holy Scriptures.*

Every trial must have a basis. The basis for the trial of Jesus was in two parts: One was the law of Moses or the first five books of the Old Testament, and the other basis was the Talmud, which is an encyclopedia and is divided into two divisions called the Mishna and the Gemara. The Mishna is an exposition of the Jewish laws and customs, the Gemara is poetry, proverbs and theology.

The five books of Moses are the source from which all Jewish customs arose. As the numbers of the Jews increased and their relationship became more complicated it became necessary to enlarge and to clarify laws, customs and legal remedies. The legal remedies and system of Jewish courts were based upon the old law where Moses told the children of Israel that they should elect judges and officers. We find this in Exodus 18:25, 26 and Deuteronomy 16:18: "Judges and officers shalt thou make thee in all thy gates, which the Lord thy God giveth thee, throughout thy tribes: and they shall judge the people with just judgment." The basis for the Great Sanhedrin was also in the law of Moses, when God told Moses to choose seventy men to stand with him before the tent of the covenant (Numbers 11:16, 17).

The Jews at the time of Jesus had three sets of courts. First, the Judges which consisted of three judges. This court could try only civil matters, and could not consider a case involving a crime. Second, there was the Lesser Sanhedrin consisting of twenty-three members which could try all kinds of cases; and third, the Great Sanhedrin sitting in Jerusalem consisting of seventy members with the High Priest. The Great Sanhedrin was composed of three sets of twenty-three members, twenty-three priests, twenty-three scribes, and twenty-three elders. The scribes were men who were learned in the law; they wrote the law out as it had to be all written out by hand. The elders were business men or executives.

The members of the Sanhedrin were thoroughly trained and conversant and linguistically perfect in all the languages of the surrounding nations as they could have no interpreter in their session. They could not be less than 40 years of age in order to belong to the Great Sanhedrin, for the reason that it took that number of years to acquaint themselves with the law of Moses and the Talmud which they had to memorize. Every member had to be married and the father of children. It was considered that a father would be more merciful.

The chairman of the Great Sanhedrin, the High Priest, was elected by the people, but at that time the high priesthood was of a political order. It was bought by the highest bidder from the Roman Governor. It was granted as a favour to those who could assist the Governor at the Imperial Court. The House of Annas was a godless and wicked aristocracy, and was guilty of the most atrocious and wicked and impious deeds. In the Sanhedrin at the trial of Jesus were Annas and Caiaphas (they seem to have both lived in the same palace), and most of the other members were sons and relatives of Annas.

According to the law the Sanhedrin could meet only in one place and that was in the Temple in a room known as the "Hall of Hewn Stones." Any other place of meeting was absolutely illegal and made their decision void and of no effect. The Sanhedrin's jurisdiction consisted of all kinds of cases. They had three ways of punishing by capital punishment or the death sentence; one was beheading for murder, burning was another; and stoning was a third method.

The Sanhedrin that sat at the trial of Jesus had plotted against Him. That was absolutely illegal. The leaders of the Jewish aristocracy were stirred up by the public and radical teaching of Jesus, while "the common people heard Him gladly." (Mark 12:37.) It was personal feeling and jealousy which set these leaders against Jesus. For instance: when they saw that He was able to heal the incurable, they tried to charge Him with witch-craft. (Matthew 9:24; 12:24; Mark 3:22; Luke 11:15.) When He told them that no Prophet was accepted in his own country, they were filled with wrath, and wanted to kill Him. (Luke 4:24-29.) This was in Nazareth of Galilee, where they had no legal right whatever to exercise the power of life and death over anyone; because the place did not contain the twenty-three Rabbis to form even a "Small Sanhedrin" or "Lesser Sanhedrin." (*Ramb. Sanhed.* 1.3; 5.2.) When He healed the man with a withered arm, they took occasion to impute to Him the Profanation of the Sabbath. (Matthew 12:9-13; Mark 3:1-6; Luke 6:6-11.) And not-withstanding His reasons that "It is lawful to save life on the Sabbath," and again, "It is lawful to do well on the Sabbath day," they joined hands with the Herodians, taking council together how they might destroy Him. When the Pharisees and

Sadducees invited Him to dine with them, all their questions were directed to catch some words out of His mouth that they might accuse Him. (Luke 11:37-57.) When He reminded them that the Temple was God's house of prayer for all people (Isaiah 56:7), but they made it a den of thieves, they sought how they might destroy Him. (Matthew 21:12-16; Mark 11:15-18; Luke 19:45-47.) They tried to entrap Him on a political catch with the hope of being able to accuse Him of treason, but they failed miserably. "Is it lawful to pay tribute to Caesar?" they asked. He answered, "Render unto Caesar that which is Caesar's and unto God that which is God's." (Matthew 22:15-21; Mark 12:13-17; Luke 20:19-25.) Their bitterest anger, however, which they could not restrain, was when He raised Lazarus (John 11:43-45); for their own eyes gave them witness to the greatness of Jesus. Their jealousy at this time found no bounds. They would have devoured Him by daylight, but could not, because of the many that believed on Him. (Matthew 21:32; John 2:23, 4:39, 50, 53, 8:31, 11:45, 12:11.) In fact they were actually hoping to kill Lazarus, who was a standing Testimony and living witness to the power and claims of Jesus (John 12:10), but they found it too dangerous, as everybody would know the reason for such an act.

They made up their mind at last, to get rid of Him under any circumstances, so long as they avoided showing their treacherous machinations, and did not excite the local multitude who believed on Him and loved Him. (Matthew 26:3-5; John 11:47-54.) Accordingly, they made arrangements with one of the weakest of His disciples, Judas Iscariot, who, like themselves, loved the mammon of this world in preference to the Lord Who bought him (Deuteronomy 32:6-18), to give him thirty pieces of silver (Matthew 27:3-9), as foretold in Jeremiah and Zechariah, that he should point out to them the place of His quiet resort with His disciples, in the middle of the night, when all the people in Jerusalem would be fast asleep.

Jesus was in the upper room with the disciples celebrating the Passover. (Luke 22:12-14.) In the midst of the ceremony while the disciples were sitting with their Master around the table Judas left them and went to the Sanhedrin and received his thirty pieces of silver. Then Jesus opened His heart to the disciples and told them that He must suffer many things of the chief priests, that He was to be crucified and that He would rise the third day. Afterwards He went with three of the disciples to Gethsemane. The hour was then approaching and there at, or soon after, midnight the multitude came consisting of chief priests, elders and officers of the Temple, and they arrested Jesus. Now it was a law at that time, based upon the old law of Moses (Deuteronomy 17:6, 7), that it was not legal for any member of the Sanhedrin to be an arresting officer. Jesus spoke to them and said, "You come to me with staves. I was daily with you in the temple." (Matthew 26:55.) It was also illegal to arrest anyone after sundown no matter how bad a criminal he was, unless he were caught in the very act. He was absolutely safe under the law, until the following day. And then he could be arrested only by the witnesses. Furthermore, Jesus was really arrested by Judas and through his instigation, which under the law was illegal, as we read in Leviticus 19:16, "Thou shalt not go up and down as a talebearer among thy people: neither shalt thou stand against the blood of thy neighbor; I am the Lord." A witness had to be a person of good character; he was forbidden to take a bribe. A Gentile could not be a witness. An accomplice or accessory could not be a witness under any circumstances. Thus Judas could neither be a witness nor arrest, because he was a companion, a traitor, "a talebearer."

According to the Mosaic and Talmudic law there was not such a thing as a Grand Jury or a preliminary hearing. Grand Juries, State's attorneys, and preliminary hearings were an abomination to the Law. To take Jesus before Annas at night to be interrogated was absolutely illegal under the law, both because it was at night, and because no one person could legally interrogate either the accused or a witness. The Examining Board of the Sanhedrin had to consist of three to seven men; no one person could independently interrogate a witness or an accused person. It was also a law that a man could not incriminate himself, in other words he could not suffer punishment or take a punishment upon his own confession; it had to be supported by the testimony of two or three witnesses. This was based on the Mosaic law, as recorded in Deuteronomy 17:6, 19:15; Numbers 35:30. Jesus knew the law and He put it right up to Annas, to whom He said: "I spoke openly to the world; I taught in the synagogue and in the temple ... Why asketh thou me? Ask them which heard me, what I have said unto them." He knew he could not be interrogated by the High Priest alone, or without his consent by the Sanhedrin. He knew further they could not support any verdict without at least two witnesses.

Aside from the illegality of the arrest and the illegality of the hearings before Annas and Caiaphas, it was illegal for the Sanhedrin to meet at night. It was illegal for them to meet until after the morning sunrise sacrifice. They were not allowed to have a trial on the day before their Sabbath. A day according to the Jewish law started at sundown and ended with the following day's sundown. Thus the arrest of Jesus and His hearing before Annas and Caiaphas was not only illegal because held at night but for the further reason that it occurred on the day before the Sabbath. Further, no trial could be held on a feast day, and as we have seen this was the Passover week, in which every day was a feast day.

Every trial before the Sanhedrin consisted of really two trials, one on one day and then on the succeeding day. Between the two trials members of the Sanhedrin had to fast and meet with one another in their homes, discussing the case from every angle, trying to find, if possible, some means to acquit the accused. After the morning sacrifice when they met in the "Hall of Hewn Stones," they would sit down for a session. There were three clerks, one would be the minute clerk for the accused, and the other the minute clerk against the accused and the third clerk who took the minutes for both sides. The accused had to stand between the two clerks and in front of the third clerk.

The witnesses would be brought before the Sanhedrin separately, but could not testify as they do now, that is, one testify to one fact and another testify to another fact. Every witness had to tell the whole story, and had to be an eye-witness of the crime from beginning to end. Each witness was first interrogated as to the date, the day and the hour, and every detail had to line up exactly true to every detail in the history of the case with every other witness as to statement of time, hour and event. If there were three witnesses and the testimony of one witness did not corroborate the others in every detail the accused would have to be found "not guilty" and set free. We find in Deuteronomy 17:6, 19:15, and Numbers 35:30 that it required more than one witness; also in Matthew 18:15 where Jesus said, "In the mouth of two or three witnesses shall every word be established." Then also they could not take any documentary evidence, for no letters could be introduced in a criminal case. Each witness had to be examined, and give his testimony separately and not in the presence of each other. He was not put under oath, for an oath was repulsive to the Jews because they could not take the name of God.

As soon as the prosecution had closed, the defendant put on his defense. After all testimony had been given came the arguments. But the Sanhedrin had to keep perfectly still until some member got up to make an argument in favor of the accused. If no one got up in his favor there could be no argument. After someone had spoken in favor of the accused, then someone also had the privilege of speaking against. Every time they spoke they had to give a valid reason for their attitude against the accused.

Then came the balloting. The High Priest could never legally express an opinion or interrogate the witness or the accused. He could never say the man was guilty or innocent. He had to keep perfectly silent. The vote of the High Priest had to be absolutely the last ballot cast, because of his high office and influence, it was felt he should not express any opinion until after the last one had spoken. No one could change his ballot from his spoken opinion unless he should change in favor of acquittal. When the balloting commenced, beginning with the youngest member of the Sanhedrin, they first took the ballots of those who voted in favor of the accused; then they took the ballots of those who were against. If everyone of the Sanhedrin voted that the accused was guilty, then by their law it would be a mistrial and the man must be set free. For, according to the Talmud, they had as one of their rules, that a man must have at least two votes in his favor, and if he did not they must set him free. There had to be a vote with a majority of two or more to find a man guilty. If the Sanhedrin were divided fifty-fifty, the accused would have to be set free. And further, a unanimous vote would set him free.

After the balloting took place they had to adjourn and the next day after fasting, prayer and conferences, and after the morning sacrifice they had a new session, for the purpose of reviewing the previous day's work and trying to find, if possible, some reason for setting free the one accused. If they were still of the same opinion after this second session, the execution had to take place immediately and before sundown. The officers of the Sanhedrin did not perform the execution. The witnesses must be the first to lay hands upon him. (Deuteronomy 17:7.) After the witnesses had laid their hands to the execution, then the people, but not the hands of the judges.

It was not necessary for the entire seventy to sit at the trial; at least twenty-three constituted and was necessary to a quorum. After Annas had interrogated Jesus He was sent to Caiaphas. We do not know if the whole Sanhedrin sat at the trial or only twenty-three. It was after midnight. Caiaphas questioned Jesus who remained silent. In angered disappointment he disregarded his duty, which of course he knew. As High Priest he could not interrogate any witness and could not express an opinion. Contrary to the law he placed Jesus under oath and he sought to interrogate Him before any witness had been interrogated. Caiaphas, illegally putting Jesus under oath, said "I adjure thee by the living God that thou tell us whether thou be the Messiah the Son of God." (Matthew 26:63.) This question Jesus would answer because He could not deny Himself and He, therefore, replied, "Thou sayest." Then the High Priest expressed himself which he had no right to do, saying, "You have heard him. He is guilty of blasphemy." (Matthew 26:65; Mark 14:63, 64; Luke 22:71.)

As we mentioned before, no one could speak against the accused until someone had spoken in his favor. There was not one favorable comment made for Jesus in that Sanhedrin; therefore, that alone should have set Him free. Legally, Jesus should have been required to make a defense as to His Messiahship, as the Jewish people were looking for the Messiah. The three wise men had come to Herod, and Herod called in the chief priests who said that the time for the Messiah was ripe. So we know that they were looking for Him, and the Sanhedrin should have interrogated Jesus as to whether He was the Messiah, the Son of God. It was their duty to have searched diligently as to whether or not these things were true, according to Deuteronomy 13:14. Having expected the Messiah, they were legally bound under the laws and rules of procedure to have taken the words of Jesus for truth until they disproved them. It was the duty of the Sanhedrin at the trial either to have disproved Him as being their Messiah or to accept as true His statement that He was the Messiah. There is no doubt that Jesus would have proven His Messiahship. The Sanhedrin violated the law on another term, when they spit in His face and struck Him. They committed physical violence. (Mark 14:65.) No judge could lay his hands on either a witness or accused, or in any way violate his person.

Another illegal act was when Caiaphas at the end of the trial rent his garment. As we read in Leviticus 21:10, "And he that is High Priest upon whose head the anointing oil was poured … to put on the garments, shall not uncover his head nor rend his clothes." The reason for this was that his priestly garment stood for the sacredness of his office.

After holding a hurried consultation together, and finding that they could not commit the murder themselves, they led Jesus away as early as possible (John 18:28) to the Judgment Hall of Pilate. (Matthew 27:1; Mark 15:1; Luke 23:1.)

How different were the crimes they asserted against Jesus when in the Supreme Judgment Hall, in the presence of the Roman Procurator! It was no longer theology, but treason against the people and the state. "We found this man perverting the people, forbidding to pay tribute to Caesar, saying that He is Himself Messiah–a king." (Luke 23:2; John 18:30.) Although they knew that the first part of the accusation was the exact opposite to His teaching, and a direct falsehood on their part; for He taught them to render to Caesar the things that are Caesar's. And when Peter was asked by the Customs Officers at Capernaum whether his Master paid tribute, he answered in the affirmative, and went there and then to Jesus to ask for the tribute money. (Matthew 17:24-27; 22:21; Mark 12:17; Luke 20:25.) But whatever they would have accused Him of would have been equally baseless, because He was "A Lamb without blemish and without spot." (1 Peter 1:19.) Yet they knew perfectly that this accusation would grip the Procurator's feelings more than any other charge, which was just what they needed. Pilate after sifting the case pronounced a verdict of not guilty, several times. (Luke 23:4; John 18:38; Matthew 27:23; Mark 15:14; Luke 23:22; John 19:4, 6.) But he had to reckon with the "multitude" who clamored for the life of Jesus. This multitude, however, did not consist of citizens of Judea, Samaria, and Galilee, who knew and loved Jesus; but were of those who came annually to the feast of the Passover, from Europe, Asia Minor, Persia, Greece, Africa, even on a larger scale than on the feast of Pentecost, as recorded in the 2nd Chapter of the Acts of the Apostles. These, while they knew that the High Priest was the chief authority in Jerusalem, scarcely ever came into touch with the life and work of Jesus. Josephus, the Jewish historian, relates (*Wars* 6:9-3), that on one of the Passover feasts, the High Priest received the count of the Passover lambs killed, which numbered no less than 256,500. As the minimum number for each lamb could not, by law, be less than 10, the number of people on that occasion must have been no less than 2,565,000, and very probably more, consisting of foreign Jews, who were ignorant about the domestic affairs of Jerusalem. These, therefore, formed the multitude which was persuaded to support the sacerdotal party before Pilate, who as a weak and vacillating creature, fearful lest they might harm him at Caesar's Court, commanded that Jesus should be crucified. (Matthew 27:20-21; Mark 15:11; Luke 23:17-19; John 18:39-40.)

We have thus shown that the trial of Jesus from beginning to end was illegal and that is the reason that there is no record of it outside of the Gospels. The Sanhedrin was afraid to keep a record for they knew that they acted illegally. In violation of the Jewish law Jesus was murdered by an unprincipled, unscrupulous, and jealous hierarchy who compelled their Roman Governor by threats, *"If thou let this man go, thou art no friend of Caesar"* (John 19:12), to uphold their action and help them carry into effect their most bloodthirsty transaction, such as the world had never seen, either before or after it. But Jesus had to die in order to make the everlasting atonement according to Leviticus 17:11, "For the life of the flesh is in the blood: and I have given it to you upon the altar to make an atonement for your souls: for it is the blood that maketh an atonement for the soul."

God demands blood to atone for sin. Man's life was forfeited and he had to die or pay the wages of death. He could not pay the penalty and live; so he wanted a substitute. Every man had sinned and could not be a substitute for his fellowman; but Messiah was sinless and could become that substitute because He has died in the room and stead of man to satisfy the law.

It was predicted that He should die, as we read in Acts 2:23, "Him being delivered by the determinate counsel and foreknowledge of God." The exact form of His death was foretold in Psalm 22. As we mentioned above the Jewish mode of a criminal's death was by stoning, but the Roman mode of execution was by crucifixion. And this Roman death was thus foretold centuries before the Romans came into power. The precious name of the spotless Son of God was to be placed on the dark roll of murderers and law breakers, as it had been written, "He was numbered with the transgressors." And those that stood by His cross and witnessed that sight of all sights beheld David's words literally fulfilled: "They pierced my hands and my feet." (Psalms 22:16.) Standing there, they gazed upon His emaciated form, and were able to "count all his bones," as the Psalmist had foretold. It had also been predicted that the soldiers who carried out the sentence of death would "gamble at the foot of the cross for His clothes," and that they would also cast lots for His inner coat, which was without seam; and so it all transpired. The exact words which fell from His parched lips had been written a thousand years before they were uttered, as in Psalm 22.

It was foretold that the Jewish authorities would appoint Him a criminal grave, but instead of which, He was "to make His grave with the rich in His death." This was done by Joseph of Arimathea, begging to be allowed to have the body of Jesus, that He might bury it in his own new tomb. Many other details of the crucifixion were minutely described and definitely stated, and every one was carried out to the very letter, as if David, Isaiah and Zechariah had really stood among that group of watchers, and had been eye-witnesses of His death at Calvary. Had they really been present at that closing scene of our Lord's life below, they could not have given a more correct and graphic account of all that transpired.

As we read their prophecies and examine the fulfillment in the Gospels, we are compelled to ask where and how did all these predictions originate, not one of which failed, or was discredited but every "*jot* and *tittle*" came to pass. Surely we can arrive at no other honest conclusion but that they came from Him Who sees the end from the beginning and Who foretells the outcome of all things before a single event transpires. What a convincing proof of the inspiration of the Bible is all this array of prophecies which so marvelously foretold in such a detailed way that miraculous birth, that matchless life, that remarkable trial, and that still more marvelous death of Him Who was sent by the Father to be the Saviour of the world, and Who of His own voluntary will came to carry out the will of God to its very letter. There could have been no collusion between the prophets who foretold these events and the apostles who recorded them, for God allowed 400 years to run their course between the prophecy of Malachi and the gospel by Matthew.

The same marvelous accuracy holds good as to our Lord's predicted resurrection, ascension, and glorification at God's right hand. And all these Old Testament Scriptures and these New Testament writings have been recorded that "we might believe that Jesus is the Messiah, the Son of God; and that, believing, we might have life through His name."

# APPENDIX V

## *The Two Deaths of Man*
### (Outline)

Not only was I an Instructor at Seattle Bible College but one year I was also a student. As a student I turned in supplementary work for the Doctrine Class (taught by veteran missionary, Reverend Ned Collingridge) dated October 20, 1967 which follows. This might help to better understand what happened to Messiah in His death. Since He was made "in every respect like His brethren," He experienced two deaths as did they.

I.  **Scriptural Testimonials as to Death**
    A.  David. **Psalm 89:47, 48**
        1.  No one escapes
        2.  No man living is excused
    B.  Solomon. **Ecclesiastes 8:8**
        1.  Agrees with David
        2.  Cannot hold back the spirit
            a.  **Hebrews 9:27**
            b.  An appointment to be met
        3.  Stalks into homes of rich & poor alike
            a.  No respecter of persons
            b.  No respecter of age

II. **Explanation**
    A.  Man is a Triune Being **1 Thessalonians 5:23**
        1.  Composed of Spirit, Soul, Body
            a.  Spirit = knows, remembers, thinks, God-conscious part of man
            b.  Soul = emotional part, feels **Psalm 107:9; Judges 10:16; Isaiah 58:10**
        2.  Body. Used by soul & spirit to execute their desire. Vehicle of expression for soul & spirit
    B.  Soul is separable from the spirit
        1.  At death the spirit leaves body **James 2:26**
        2.  At death the soul leaves the body **1 Kings 17:21-22; Genesis 35:18**

### III. Where are the "Dead"?

A. Soul Departs the Body
  1. To *Gehenna* = torment **Luke 16**
  2. Righteous to *Paradise*, "Abraham's Bosom"
  3. Prior to His crucifixion Messiah told His disciples about that place
    a. 3 days & 3 nights *in the **heart** of the earth.* **Matthew 12:40**
    b. His body in tomb on *surface* of the earth. **Acts 2:27 & 31**
  4. It is recorded **Ephesians 4:8-10**
    a. He descended to lower parts of the earth
    b. Led out a multitude of captives
    c. To thief, ***Today in Paradise*** = "pleasure garden")
    d. *"Into thy hands I commend my **spirit**"* He gave up the ***ghost*** (spirit) Luke 23:46
      1) Body on the cross
      2) Spirit left for Paradise
      3) Preached (proclaimed, heralded) to the (righteous) spirits in prison (*sheol*)
      4) They heard and saw Him
      5) All five senses operative
  5. Before Messiah arose
    a. Hollow place in center of earth
      1) *Sheol* OT means place of departed spirits *Intermediate state*
      2) NT is called *Hades*
    b. Same terms used to describe Eternity of God
      1) Used to describe eternity of torment (fire) **Matthew 25:41, 46** *everlasting punishment*
      2) Righteous = *eternal life*
  6. After Messiah arose
    a. Paradise is "up" **2 Corinthians 12:2-4**
      1) Where the Lord is
      2) Paradise section removed from center of earth (*sheol*)
    b. Paul said: *"To be absent from the body is to be present with the Lord."* **2 Corinthians 5:6-8**
  7. Messiah teaches disciples of place of departed:
    a. **Luke 16:19-31**
    b. Place of conscious existence

B. Intermediate State
   1. When spirit-soul leaves the body, the BODY called "dead"
      a. It is "asleep" **John 11:11-14; 1 Thessalonians 4:13**
      b. Body asleep–knows not anything **Ecclesiastes 9:5**
   2. Spirit-soul still alive when departing body
      a. There is a place for the body
      b. There is a place for the soul
   3. God's Word final authority
      a. Moses died–body buried
         1) Soul departed–alive
         2) 1,500 years later appeared on Mt. with Messiah **Luke 9:28-31**
         3) Not body of earthly flesh–but celestial body with eyes, ears, nose, etc. recognized, talked
      b. I AM the God of Abraham, Isaac, Jacob
         1) At burning bush to Moses **Exodus 3:6**
         2) Jesus repeated this and added: *"God is not the God of the **dead**, but of the **living**."* **Matthew 22:32**
         3) Abraham dead **330** years when God first said I AM. Isaac dead **225** years. Jacob dead **198** years. Messiah implied that, though these had fallen "asleep," yet they were **LIVING**. He is the God of the LIVING!

## IV. Why Two Deaths of Man?
   A. Entered because of sin
      1. **Genesis 2:27**
         a. Spiritual death–separated from God–expelled from the Garden
         b. Physical death came to them eventually
      2. **Romans 5:12**
   B. Remedy is Messiah
      1. Man under curse of the law because of sin
         a. Physical and spiritual death
         b. On all mankind
      2. Messiah was made a curse **Galatians 3:13**
         a. Messiah died **2 deaths**
         b. **Isaiah 53:9** *buried with the rich in His **death*** (plural in Hebrew)
         c. Forsaken of God, He quoted **Psalm 22:1** Separation from God is *spiritual death*
         d. He gave up the ghost–His spirit separated from His body **James 2:26** *physical death*

# The Existence of the Body
## After Death and the Resurrection

*"For we know that if our earthly house of this tabernacle were dissolved, we have a building of God, an house not made with hands, eternal in the heavens"* (2 Corinthians 5:1).

This tells of hope for the eternal resurrection body. The earthly or physical body will be *dissolved* ( the word associated with death) meaning "to loosen down," "to disintegrate," "to make useless," "come to naught," "destroy." The Greek word for "destroy" does not mean that the earthly body will be entirely annihilated–to be no more–but that it will put on a more perfect tabernacle at the Resurrection. Our present body is subject to physical death but the body or "house" God will give us at the first resurrection will not ever be subject to death for that body or "house not made with hands" is eternal in the heavens. (*Eternal* here is the same word used to describe the everlasting existence of God.) We can be (confident)–of good courage (2 Corinthians 5:6-8) and not dread death or the dissolution of this earthly body for we will receive a better body, a house or building from heaven.

The words "destroyed," "dissolved" do not mean annihilated (that they are no more), even as a glass is destroyed but its parts are still in existence. Even as an automobile is destroyed, all its parts are still "around," etc. So this earthly house or physical body, though dissolved (destroyed) by death, still continues in existence and at the coming of Messiah will be raised, reunited with the soul-spirit which went on to heaven, and changed or fashioned like His glorious body. See 1 Thessalonians 4:13-17; 1 Corinthians 15:51-54.

In this verse then (2 Corinthians 5:1) we see that there is a body for the redeemed man or woman after physical death and the resurrection–that it is a body made by God, and that it is eternal!

An important question often has been raised concerning the condition of those in heaven. Will they sorrow if they see what is happening to their loved ones on earth? The Scriptures tell us that there will be no sorrow, grief, sadness or tears in heaven for we will have *glorified* bodies at the resurrection which do not have any *earthly* emotion! What does it mean that "God will wipe away all tears from their eyes"? (Revelation 7:17.) Will there be actual tears for God to wipe away? This refers to that sorrow or grief that *caused* tears when we were on earth. Those in heaven will completely forget that their sinful loved ones ever lived! *"The **righteous** shall be in everlasting remembrance"* (Psalm 112:6). This strongly implies that the **wicked** will *not* be in everlasting remembrance. Even the *mother* (the *womb*) shall forget her *sinful* son as we read in Job 24:19-20!

# BIBLIOGRAPHY

Cohen, The Reverend Dr. A. M.A., Ph.D., D.H.L. *The Soncino Chumash*. London, The Soncino Press, 1956.

——. *Everyman's Talmud*. New York, Schocken Books, 1949.

Davis, J.D. *Westminster Dictionary of the Bible*. Philadelphia, Westminster Press, c1944.

DeHaas, Jacob, (ed.) *The Encyclopedia of Jewish Knowledge*, New York, Behrman's Jewish Book House, 1946.

Edersheim, Alfred. *The Life and Times of Jesus the Messiah, Vol. I & II*. New York, Longman's, Green and Company, 1904.

Edidin, Ben. *Jewish Holidays and Festivals*. New York, Hebrew Publishing Company, c1941.

Enelow, H.G. *A Jewish View of Jesus* New York, Bloch Publishing Company, 1931.

Freehof, Solomon B. *Preface to Scripture*. Cincinnati, Ohio, Union of American Hebrew Congregations, c1950.

Gift, Joseph L. *Life and Customs of Jesus' Time*. Cincinnati, Ohio, The Standard Publishing Foundation, c1947.

Gilbert, Arthur and Oscar Tarcov. *Your Neighbor Celebrates*. New York, Friendly House, c1957.

Goldstein, David. *Jewish Panorama*. St. Paul, Minnesota, Radio Replies Press, c1940 by David Goldstein.

Grant, F.C. *Ancient Judaism and the New Testament*. New York, Macmillan Co., 1959.

Heller, Abraham Mayer. *The Vocabulary of Jewish Life*. New York, Hebrew Publishing Company, c1942.

Kertzer, Rabbi Morris N. *What is a Jew?* New York, The Macmillan Company, 1960.

Klinck, Arthur W. *Home Life in Bible Times*. St. Louis, Missouri, Concordia, 1947.

Orr, James (general editor). *International Standard Bible Encyclopaedia*, Grand Rapids, Eerdmans c1939.

Powell, Frank J. *The Trial of Jesus Christ*. Grand Rapids, Michigan, Wm. B. Eerdmans Publishing Co., c1948, The Paternoster Press.

Rosenau, William. *Jewish Ceremonial Institutions and Customs*. New York, Bloch Publishing Co., c1925 by W. Rosenau.

Sabiers, Karl G., *Where Are the Dead?* Los Angeles, California. Robertson Publishing Co., c1940.

Whiston, A.M. (trans.). *The Life and Works of Flavius Josephus, Antiquities of the Jews*. Philadelphia, The John C. Winston Company, n.d.

# General Index